your
THREE-YEAR-
OLD

your
THREE-YEAR-
OLD

Friend or Enemy

by Louise Bates Ames
and Frances L. Ilg

Gesell Institute of Child Development

Illustrated with photographs

DELACORTE PRESS/NEW YORK

First printing

Designed by Giorgetta Bell McRee

LIBRARY OF CONGRESS CATALOGING IN PUBLICATION DATA

Ames, Louise Bates.
Your three-year-old.

Bibliography: p.
Includes index.
1.   Child development.   2.   Children—Management.
3.   Child psychology.
I.   Ilg, Frances Lillian, 1902–   joint author.
II.   Gesell Institute of Child Development, New Haven.
III.   Title.
HQ772.5.A399   649'.123   76-8466
ISBN 0-440-09883-1

Photo credits appear on page 168

To our daughters,
Joan and Tordis,

and our grandchildren,
Carol, Clifford, Karl, and Whittier

CONTENTS

chapter one
CHARACTERISTICS OF THE AGE

Just as the tides have their rhythms, so does human behavior have its own predictable rhythms. As the child grows older, "good" ages alternate with "bad"; times of equilibrium alternate with times of disequilibrium; and periods when behavior tends to be expansive and outgoing alternate with periods when everything seems to be pulled in.

It should come as no surprise, then, to the mother or father of a rambunctious Two-and-a-half-year-old, that sometime around the age of Three their son or daughter does seem to calm down conspicuously. He says "yes" instead of "no"; "will" instead of "won't." He smiles instead of frowns, laughs instead of cries, gives in comfortably to your requests instead of resisting them.

Around thirty-three months of age, many children go through a stage of reliving their babyhood, of thinking about themselves in terms of their own past. The child may pretend that he is a baby, even going back to the use of baby talk, though some are loath to give up their glorious acquisition of speech. So, a child may say, "I'm a little baby. I can't walk, I have no teeth, I drink from a bottle. But I *can* talk."

However, by Three, most have caught up with themselves chronologically and are now in a state of equilibrium and of no longer looking back. In fact, by Three, many children seem to be developing a rather good self-concept, seem to have a solid set of feelings about themselves. There is little question that this sense of self is influenced by the way others treat them.

At thirty months the opposition of "I" and "you" was so strong that there seemed to be a chasm between them, with the opposition of "Me do it myself" when he really could not, and "You do it" when he actually could do a thing himself. But at Three years of age the chasm seems to be bridged by that delightfully cooperative word "we."

In fact, Three is a highly "we" age. The child likes to say "let's," as "Let's go for a walk, shall we?" The sense of togetherness or "we-ness" seems to make him depend on the adult and makes him lean on him or her, though he also enjoys the sense of sharing. The very child who has been so independent earlier may now ask his mother: "Help me," "Show me."

But even though the increased maturity of Three allows him sometimes to share or even lean instead of resisting, as earlier, Three is also aware of and proud of his increasing maturity and increasing ability. He frequently asks, after some particular display of prowess, "Could a baby do this?"

Dr. Arnold Gesell has described Three as a "coming of age, a time at which the many strands of previous development converge, and a new self comes into focus." The conflicting extremes of six months ago give way to a high degree of smoothness, integration, and self-control. Emotions are well in hand.

Three seems, for all his relative immaturity, to be rather highly aware of what other people like and do not like. In fact, many seem quite able to tell whether another person is happy or sad, pleased or angry, by watching that person's face.

At any rate, the typical Three-year-old wants to please. He wants to do things "right." "Do it dis way?" he may ask hopefully. He is highly susceptible to praise and fav-

orable comment and also highly responsive to friendly humor.

The increased smoothness seen in the typical child of Three has a strongly motor basis. His body is now delightfully at his command. It does not surprise him with inadequacy as it has done in the past and will do again in another six months or so, when *motor* insecurity seems to lie at the basis of much of the marked *emotional* insecurity the Three-and-a-half-year-old exhibits.

Three is sure and nimble on his feet. He walks well, and he runs easily. He can turn sharp corners without elaborate preparation and precaution. His motor sureness is evident even as he walks. He no longer stretches his arms out for balance but instead walks securely and swings his arms with ease.

Three now enjoys other children, but most of all he enjoys his mother. He loves to do things with her—go for a walk, go to the store, "help" with housework, and, above all, play. He is happiest when his mother finds it possible to give up other activities and concentrate on him. Almost anything the two of you do together brings him joy. It is bliss to have Mother read to him, play games with him, talk to him, just be near him.

Emotionally, it is fair to assume, the typical Three-year-old is a rather happy person—calm, collected, secure and capable, friendly and giving. He conforms easily, and thus, liking to please, he pleases.

Not only is he secure physically and happy socially and calm emotionally, but language now means a great deal to him. He *loves* new words—new words, big words, different words. He loves such words as "surprise," "new," "different," "secret." Even when a situation may seem to be beginning to deteriorate, it is often quite possible to pull things together by the use of just the right word. And if the word is "surprise," and if it is accompanied by an actual physical surprise (no more than a cracker or cookie will usually do), the young child's delight is truly rewarding to the provider of this delicious occasion.

And then, just as you are really beginning to enjoy this tractable little creature, growth forces push your child's behavior a little farther along in their ever-evolving cycle, and he hits Three-and-a-half, a wild and wonderful age with characteristics all its own. As at other times in life, an age of disequilibrium follows an age of equilibrium. (*See* Figure 1.)

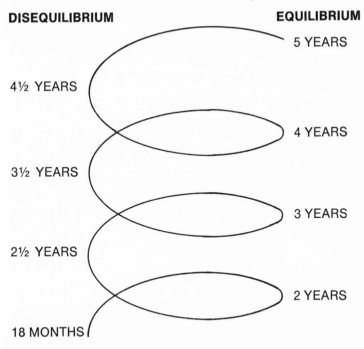

Figure 1
Alternation of Ages of Equilibrium and Disequilibrium

Three is a conforming age. Three-and-a-half is just the opposite. Refusing to obey is perhaps the key aspect of this turbulent, troubled period in the life of the young child. It sometimes seems to his mother that his main concern is to strengthen his will, and he strengthens this will by going against whatever is demanded of him by that still most important person in his life, his mother.

Many a mother discovers that even the simplest event or occasion can elicit total rebellion. Dressing, eating, going to the bathroom, getting up, going to bed—whatever the routine, it can be the scene and setting for an

5

all-out, no-holds-barred fight. Techniques and tricks formerly useful can no longer be guaranteed to work. The mother's equally resistant response may be tempered by knowing that soon, when he is Four, her child will have developed a self-concept strong enough so that he can sometimes conform, and also that he will sometimes enjoy going out-of-bounds and saying and doing things he knows full well will not be permitted. But even when out-of-bounds at Four, he will usually be much less difficult to manage than now, at Three-and-a-half.

You may not need much help and advice when your child is Three. When he is Three-and-a-half you may need all the help you can get, and then some! Since forewarned is forearmed, we shall tell you here about some of the things you may expect to experience when your child reaches the admittedly somewhat difficult age of forty-two months.

We may fairly, and in all friendliness, describe the Three-and-a-half-year-old boy or girl as being characteristically inwardized, insecure, anxious, and, above all, determined and self-willed. One might assume that his strong-willed self-assertiveness, which is so conspicuously evident, might be rooted in a strong personal security. Not so! In fact, the very opposite seems to be the case.

The Three-and-a-half-year-old child seems emotionally very insecure from the word go. This insecurity is even shown in physical ways. He stutters. He stumbles. He trembles. A child who six months earlier may have walked a proud one-foot-to-a-step up the stairs may now go back to a more babyish two-feet-to-a-step. Quite steady at Three, he may now express fear of falling. Steady-handed at Three as he built a sturdy tower of blocks, his hands may now tremble as he adds blocks to his tower. Handedness may even shift at this age, and it may seem as if the child actually does not know which hand to use.

Stuttering, which in many comes in at this age (though a very early talker may already have stuttered as early as Two-and-a-half, that earlier age of disequilibrium),

causes many parents undue anxiety. We ourselves tend to label stuttering at this age as mere "preschool non-fluency" and unless it prolongs itself for several months, let it go at that.

Actually, tensional outlets of all sorts are conspicuous at this age. The child may suck his thumb, bite his nails, pick his nose, rub his genitals, chew on his clothes. And he may well hang onto his security blanket as onto life itself.

Vision, too, may pose special problems. Not only does the child fear heights, but he often complains that he cannot see when he is being read to in a group. He wants to be right on top of the book and often holds his picture book very close if he is looking at it by himself. He does best being read to alone, preferably sitting on the reader's lap so that he can adjust the book and see it at his preferred visual distance.

Emotional insecurity as well as physical insecurity is commonly expressed at this often difficult age. Sometimes it almost seems that nothing pleases. Three-and-a-half attempts to control his environment in ways that will, perhaps, make him feel more secure, more sure of himself. "Don't look," "Don't laugh," "Don't talk," he commands those around him. But, in his immaturity, he is often inconsistent. "Don't look," he may order at one minute, and at the next may become very angry if not given full attention. He may then insist that *all* attention be focused on himself and may feel left out if it is not. He may refuse to let Father read his paper, or Mother chat on the phone, or Mother and Father talk to each other.

He is developing a deepening sense of himself in relation to, but also as apart from, others and thus is not as interested in the concept of "we" as he was just earlier. This may be at least in part what leads to those bossy demands of "Don't laugh" or "Don't look." He seems to feel invaded even by other people's glances.

In fact, the child of this age makes his parents walk a real tightrope. This is done to the extent that some mothers, even those quite skilled at parenting, find their greatest success by turning their child over to a baby-sitter. It can be rather frustrating to an experienced and normally effective mother to see a young baby-sitter doing better with her child than she. But the fact seems to be that Three-and-a-half is amazingly sensitive to the reactions of others. He *knows* that the sitter really doesn't *care* whether he eats or goes hungry, gets his rest or becomes exhausted. With exquisite sensitiveness he deals out the grief to the person who *does* care, his mother. No mother of a child of this age should hesitate to place the burden of daily routines on the shoulders of a sitter, who, for the time being, may be the best person for the task.

Inconsistency is also expressed in the emotional extremes of this interesting age. The child may seem to be extremely shy at one minute and overbold the next. Inconsistent, and determined to control the adult, he can make things difficult since he must—but definitely must—have his own way about almost everything. And he is surprisingly firm in enforcing his own demands. If, while out for a walk, he decides that he will not go any farther, he will stand stock-still. If you walk away, assuming that your departure will motivate him to follow, you can continue on until he is but a speck in the distance. He will not budge.

Or, he will set up a "nothing-pleases-me" situation in which, as when taken shopping, he does not want to go into the store, but at the same time refuses to stay in the car, and will howl bloody murder whichever alternative you choose. (This behavior should give the parent the clue that shopping should be avoided at the time of day when the child must be taken along. Hopefully, if no sitter is available, mothers might take turns with other mothers in the neighborhood in taking care of those children who do not do well in stores.)

Yet, for all of this, the child's frequent "me too" suggests that he thinks he is, or at least wants to be, as big and capable as anybody else, and wants to do what others are doing.

Routines seem to give him the most trouble. Mealtime and dressing may be two of the most difficult routines. Each bite, each garment, may provoke a full-fledged battle. During the smoother parts of the day—between routines—he may be loving and amusing, his most delightful self. Warm, friendly, appealing, affectionate and confiding, creative and delightful he can be at such times.

It may be hard for you to imagine that, only minutes

before, you and he may have been locked in mortal combat about whether he would or would not eat his lunch. If he wants to, this child can be a real joy and delight— at least for brief periods. He can show imagination, inventiveness, and a real capacity for play. He can be aware of the other person's feelings and can be extremely endearing as he expresses his own affections.

But emotionally, if one is to judge by the child's behavior, Three-and-a-half can be a time of great stress and strain. Insecure within himself, yet determined to dominate, the child of this age has great difficulty in managing his turbulent emotions. Life is a struggle, and emotions, much of the time, seem to give little pleasure. Happily, six months more time may see your child at a point where his emotions, though strong and even violent, can be a source of emotional pleasure and satisfaction for him.

Friends are extremely important even at this early age. In fact, it may be the child's enthusiasm about his friends that represents one of the most delightful aspects of his behavior.

This is the age above all others when many children enjoy the company of one or more imaginary companions. These may be imaginary people or imaginary animals. One boy we knew had a whole family of imaginary bears. These bears took up so much room in the house, or in the family car, that there was hardly space for the rest of the (real) family.

Some children, instead of enjoying an imaginary companion, pretend that they are someone other than themselves. They may play the role of a cat, or a dog, or a pony. Also, some companions are weak and easily bossed around by the child. Others are bossy and extremely demanding.

If the Three-year-old can sometimes be thought of as a watcher and a waiter, the Three-and-a-half-year-old, for all his anxiety and difficulty, is much more an actor and a doer. There is a suddenness and vigor about his behavior that is rather striking, though not always comfortable. He may suddenly wet his pants, surprising even himself; or he may suddenly burst out crying when things do not go his way.

Many of the behaviors that characteristically occur at Three-and-a-half are admittedly somewhat worrisome to, and difficult for, the parent. One aspect of the age that is more welcome is the marked developmental spurt that occurs now. Some children who have been developing slowly, or somewhat atypically, do at this age show a marked spurt that, happily, brings their behavior pretty much up to that which is customarily expected at this age. This can be especially true of late-talking boys, many of whom, rather suddenly around the age of Three-and-a-half, start speaking fluently and effectively.

In fact, for any child, the increasingly effective verbal ability that expresses itself around this time can be one of the more satisfactory aspects of behavior. Not only does vocabulary continue to increase, but the child now uses his language as an interesting means of real communication, in contrast to the Two-and-a-half-year-old's more limited "Me-do-it-myself" kind of conversation. And, an increased interest in books and storytelling provides much happy time for both parent and child.

The child's plan to marry the parent of the opposite sex is one of his amusing verbalizations. One little boy, who was planning to marry his mother, was asked by her, "What shall we do after we are married?" "We'll sit on a sofa and talk very softly, and sometimes we won't talk at all," was his touching reply.

WARNING!

While you and your child are enjoying the brief honeymoon that Three years of age often brings, you will scarcely need any warnings. When he or she reaches the more difficult time of Three-and-a-half, we would like to give two suggestions.

The first is that, as we have tried to emphasize, even though he may be difficult at times, *your child is not your enemy. It is not you against him.* He fights you, when he does, because that is the way his mind and body work at this age. You will need to require many things of him just to get him through a normal day. He does need to get up and go to bed; to be dressed and undressed; to go to the bathroom and be fed.

Such occasions may require that he comply with your wishes to a certain extent. Do not unnecessarily multiply the occasions when *your* will must prevail. Stay out of conflict when you can. Even let *him* win at times.

Our second suggestion, as at all ages, is that you remember that every child is an individual. Not all children behave alike. Nor do they all reach the customary stages of development at the same time. Your own particular boy or girl may reach the behavior stages we describe as being characteristic of Three and of Three-and-a-half either early or late. Or, indeed, he or she may live through these ages in ways quite other than those we describe.

You might conceivably have a child who is comfortable within himself and easy to be with at all ages, including the usually difficult age of Three-and-a-half. So, don't worry if your own child does *not* express the dangers and difficulties we have described. But if he does, you may take comfort in the fact that often the most highly endowed children *do* express the extremes of both the easy and the difficult ages.

The descriptions we give in this book merely portray the way that children of these ages *often* behave. We hope they will be of help to you. But if your child behaves otherwise, don't worry. Not every child goes through all the standard stages, and even those who do, have their own individual timetables. They may quite benignly be ahead of, or behind, or different from, the so-called *average*.

chapter two
THE CHILD WITH OTHER CHILDREN

THE THREE-YEAR-OLD

One of the great joys of life for the child as he moves on through the older preschool years is other children. This joy is rather later in coming than many parents anticipate. It is often disappointing to young parents that their Eighteen-monther or their Two-year-old shows such a marked tendency to *ignore* other children with whom they have hoped he would play happily. At Two-and-a-half, the child does pay a lot of attention to others, but much of his attention is spent in protecting the things he wants to play with *from* these other children, and in grabbing what the other children have.

Happily, all that you have been waiting for in the direction of your child's playing nicely with others may come to you when your boy or girl turns Three. Children of this age, even though still rather immature in their social reactions, tend to be extremely enthusiastic about other children. "We" is a favorite word, and "friend" is coming into the child's vocabulary. And the air may ring with "Me, too." In a nursery school setting, for the very first time, a child may devote as much attention, and as much verbalization, to other children as to his teacher. (*See* Figure 2.)

Cooperative play now begins to take the place of parallel play—that is, the child actually plays *with* another child instead of merely beside him, as formerly. Children seem less selfish than just earlier, and many not only can share possessions with others but can themselves use some of the preschool "techniques" used earlier by

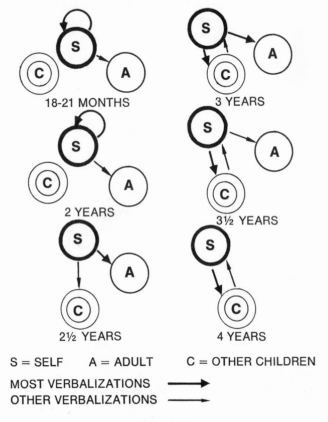

18-21 MONTHS

3 YEARS

2 YEARS

3½ YEARS

2½ YEARS

4 YEARS

S = SELF   A = ADULT   C = OTHER CHILDREN

MOST VERBALIZATIONS

OTHER VERBALIZATIONS

Figure 2
Person to Whom the Child Talks Most

teachers. Thus, a child may be able to persuade another child, who wants to grab his toy, that *something else* might be just as acceptable.

Or, a child may accept another child's statement of ownership: "That's *my* truck!" "Oh, that's your truck?" Or, a child may say, "Let me have yours, and you have mine. That would be a good thing."

Often, in fact, instead of a nursery school teacher's needing to solve some little squabble, a third child (if accepted as a friend and leader by both the others) may come up with a solution to a social problem. Or, children sometimes ask permission of each other: "May I play with you?," "Could I use that now, please?"

In fact, at Three, many children are beginning to be interested in other children's feelings, in how things seem to others. The adult can sometimes solve small squabbles by helping a child to see the way things look from the other person's point of view, something that would have been quite beyond him six months earlier.

Some children, indeed, have very special friends and really look forward to, and enjoy, playing with these special friends.

Child-child behavior is now extremely different from what it was at Two-and-a-half. More is going on, and more *different* things are going on. Children are responding at more different levels, so that the impression of unity in a room where a group of children is playing, so strong at Two, is no longer felt.

Three is, on occasion, not above mere indiscriminate wandering around a room without relating to much of anybody. Or, one child may play alone with dolls or paint or clay. Another may be engaged in conversation with any adult present, showing something, telling something, or asking for help. Another may be playing near some other child, merely watching, asking permission, cooperating, or being aggressive. Three or four others may be engaged in quiet conversation or activity in the doll corner or with big blocks. Two others may be slamming things around, climbing, screaming, or laughing at their own noisy activity

Thus activity in any one group of children ranges from

solitary play, to conversation with an adult, to aggressive play between two children, to relatively cooperative play between two or more. There are many different kinds of subgroups and different degrees of cooperation.

And, whatever any given child may be doing at any moment, activity and groupings shift very rapidly. Play for many still seems rather individual, but now they seem to like to be at least physically near others. There is relatively little physically isolated play. But there is also little structure or continuity to groupings, as any one child may shift from climbing, to house building, to clay, to paint, very rapidly.

Behavior shifts not only from place to place and from type to type, but also as to level of maturity. A group that is cooperatively building a block house, or is nicely engaged in domestic play, may suddenly stop to pull, tug, hit, push, or kick to get an object for self, reinforcing physical action with cries of "It's mine!"

In fact, children may still seem a little more comfortable with adults than with other children. For the most part, they approach any adult present with requests for help or information or to show an object or activity. But with other children a conversational relationship still may not be entirely sure or comfortable, and any conversation or imaginative play may quite suddenly degenerate into horseplay, loud laughter, or silly joking, even when fights over ownership do not interrupt its smoothness.

For the most part, children are now more interested *in each other* than in any particular activity. A group working around the clay table may watch each other with interest. (Though some still ignore others.) Or, a child calls the attention of others to what he has made, instead of merely showing it to an adult, as earlier. In some small groupings there is almost continuous and fairly subtle interpersonal relation. And when it comes to boy-girl couples, one sees the beginning of sometimes rather flirtatious approaches.

Greatly increased maturity is now shown by the fact

that some children can use sharing or turn-taking techniques spontaneously: "When I'm finished—OK?" Or, in a game of trains, a boy may suggest that a friend go *around* him. When the friend refuses, the first boy adjusts even further and goes around *him*.

Or, one girl may suggest to another, "You get another train. I need this one." But then she may make no further protest if the other girl holds onto the train. That is, children seem less aggressive and defensive than at Two-and-a-half, and more interested in *solutions* about property fights than in the fights themselves. Altercations are more easily solved than earlier, both because children are beginning to use techniques such as asking permission and taking turns, and because their own intentions are more flexible and not so rigidly adhered to as just earlier.

Much conversation is social and friendly, having to do with the carrying out of real or imaginary play activity: "Make b'lieve this is a boat," "You're a doggy. Say 'Bow-wow,'" "Have some cake." Much conversation is self-initiated, but many now do converse, meaningfully, with others. They may give or withhold permission, make a reciprocal offer when something is offered to them, take part in rather complex imaginary housekeeping or other group play. Or, they could be playing with clay (or other material) but talking about when they were babies.

Though there are often groupings of three or four or even more, in general twosomes work out best. With more than two, unexpected difficulties or misunderstandings or sudden shifts of interest all interfere with smooth prolonged interchange. And even with only two, some still seem most comfortable at parallel play rather than at the beginnings of cooperative play. There can be some good individual play, such as when a girl carefully sets the table in the doll corner, or wheels and tends her doll baby.

Cooperative play still tends to be so rudimentary that if an older child—say, a Four-year-old—is present, it may be difficult for him to find a point of contact. Thus two frequently play together but do not *do* very much. Both may just stand inside their "store" with heads out of the "store window," being "storekeepers." That is, having set up a cooperative play situation, they often do not *do* much with it.

There is now definitely less aggression than at Two-and-a-half but more excluding. Six months later, this tendency will be more extreme, but it is beginning here. Excluding is firm, and both physical and verbal, but not consistent. The ones who are doing the excluding may put up a brave front, but it can easily be broken down. The ones excluded usually persist for a while, and then, if not successful, turn to an adult for help. Interpersonal relations are still tentative and experimental. Children seem interested in the behavior of others even when the others are excluding them.

Attempts at influencing other children vary from physically pulling them out of a chair, to a fierce and verbal, "Dat's mine. Get out of here!," to friendly words, such as, "Let's go down in that old house."

THE THREE-AND-A-HALF-YEAR-OLD

By this time, when children are together, there is very little isolated play. Most are involved in groups of possibly only two or three, but often more, in rather elaborate, long-continued cooperative play. There may be only two or three groups in an entire nursery school playroom, involving all the children, but the makeup of these groups is often rather fluid.

Children now seem as much interested in each other as individuals as in what each does or says. Play is beginning to be definitely cooperative. There is much less squabbling over materials than earlier, and children may show not only deference to each other's wishes but also actual interest in and admiration for what others are doing. And when opposite sexes are involved there can even be a certain amount of smiling and flirtation.

In play involving cooperation, there is much give-and-
take: "Shall I?" "Do this?" "Don't do that," "Let's do this
and that." Children talk, act, smile, cooperate, tantalize,
flirt. They seem to enjoy their imaginative activity and
their relations with each other, often as much as the
manipulation of materials.

There is in boys considerable silly clowning and many
foolish antics. One boy may run around in a conspicuously
silly way, and others laugh at him or imitate him. Even
in girls, rather high-level cooperative play can break down
at any time if children are not well matched or nicely
motivated.

Play may be structured by the situation (as when several children are painting, or working with clay at a table) but often it is structured more by minimum props and the children's own imagination.

Children at this age not only play together with paint and clay and carts and tricycles, but also with nice imaginative play, largely self-initiated. They are beginning to enjoy prolonged doll play, playing house, building structures with blocks. Many now spontaneously verbalize their own role in imaginative play: "I'm the store man," "I'm the fire truck man sitting in the house watching the fire engines go by."

Cooperative play can now be quite delightful in its complexity, especially since verbal imagining combines with real action to hold things together. Children may talk about what they are doing or are going to do—actually doing more talking than acting things out. For instance, a group of boys may pretend that they are all animals in a zoo. They may talk about this in some detail, changing roles from time to time, without actually having the animals *do* much of anything.

However, boys, especially, may act more than they talk. Thus, several may build a "firehouse" and then all take turns jumping off this firehouse. Or, all may stand and make "fire-siren" noises.

Friendships may become even stronger and more intense than at Three. But for all the interest children show in each other, except for certain pairs of strong friends, the membership of groups is by no means constant. Any one child may break off from one group to join another.

Perhaps unfortunately, at this age many define friendships by excluding those children whom they do *not* like from their games: "We don't want him," "We don't like her," "She can't play with us" are phrases that ring out all too often. It is as if children emphasize similarity or liking by excluding those who are dissimilar or disliked.

Earlier, if children did not play together, it was mostly because they had not reached the level of maturity that

would permit group play. Now, if they do not play together, it may be because two or three are pointedly and definitely excluding a certain child from their group.

Often a teacher or mother can overcome this initial exclusion by offering some role that the newcomer may play: "He's the mailman with the mail," "He's the milkman bringing you the milk," "She's the grandmother, come to visit." Certainly we as adults will work to see that in a play group no child is conspicuously and hurtfully excluded. But we should not blame children (or their parents) when they do exclude. The in-group tends to be very strong.

Interest in people as opposed to objects has increased

to the point that children are often able to solve their own squabbles over materials by offering substitute materials or by suggesting turns or even by agreeing (themselves) to wait or to use something else. But play, though varied, lively, and enthusiastic, may not hold up for long periods. Quarrels develop, or fatigue or boredom sets in. Thus, some adult, either mother, baby-sitter, or teacher, needs to be in the near vicinity to step in when intervention is needed.

That children are extremely important to other children at this age is suggested by a study of our own, in a nursery school setting, in which Three-and-a-half was the very first age when children directed more attention and more talk to other children than to their teacher. (*See* Figure 2, page 14.)

SIBLINGS

Three-year-olds are often, much of the time, pleasant and friendly. They seem to find it easy to get on with other people, siblings as well as children outside the family. Three-and-a-half-year-olds are often more thorny. They want their own way, and they find it quite difficult to adapt.

Depending partly on temperament (their own as well as the temperaments of their brothers and sisters) and partly on the family situation, they may find it easy or difficult to get on with others in the family.

If a Three-year-old has been the only one for some time, and has perhaps been somewhat favored and pampered, the arrival of a baby sibling, and the sibling itself, may be looked on with considerable disfavor. He may very likely suggest that you take the baby back, or make even more adverse comments as to how he feels about Baby. On the other hand, many are friendly and warm and helpful with baby brother or sister.

This should come as no surprise. Reasonable tact and a watchful eye should be enough to avoid major confrontations.

When in a good mood and when things are going well for him, Three may get along very nicely with older siblings. If he is in a bad mood and things are going badly for him, he will quarrel with sibs as with anybody else.

Your best bet here, as at any age, if a good deal of quarreling takes place, is to figure out what times of day or what kinds of situations seem to cause the most trouble, and then to avoid them if you can. Separation works wonders. Most important of all, try to appreciate that brothers and sisters for the most part fight with each other because they enjoy it. Even when they scream the loudest, there is a certain satisfaction. So, if quarreling bothers you, try to stop it, but at least accept the fact that most any brothers and sisters of any age do fight with each other at least part of the time.

chapter three
TECHNIQUES

As at every age, the very best techniques you can use to help your child behave as you wish are those tailored to fit the strong points, and the weak ones, of the age itself. Thus, the more you know about any age—especially one of the more difficult ones—the more effectively you can fashion your own techniques to match both the age and also the special personality of your own individual child.

When your child is Three, hopefully, you will not be in need of so very many techniques. Life tends to flow quite smoothly for the usual child at this age, and normal parental enthusiasm, stamina, goodwill, ingenuity, and common sense may be all that are needed.

Not so at Three-and-a-half. The child of this age tends to be *very* hard to handle. It is important to keep in mind, at a time like this, that your child is not your enemy. Those times when a child is at his *worst* are often the times when he needs the *most* help from you. He is not behaving as he does just to be naughty. He is behaving as he does because that is the way his physical self functions at this time in his life. He really cannot help being the way he is, so it is *you* who have to help him.

What can you do to help things go smoothly for both of you?

First of all, accept the fact that at this age the child's

big emotional struggle is with his mother. She is the one who matters supremely to him. She is the one he needs to conquer. Almost any young child is at his best but also at his worst with his own mother. Never more so than now.

Recognizing this fact, you will if at all possible enlist the services of a good baby-sitter for as much of the time as possible. As we've said before, it may be somewhat deflating to see an untrained high school girl lead your son or daughter smoothly through routines that you, the mother, cannot manage. But that is the way it is.

Why? Because the sitter really *does not care* deeply if your child fails to dress properly or go to bed quickly. The Three-and-a-half-year-old fights *only* with a worthy opponent—his mother.

This advice may seem like the all-time cop-out. It remains our best advice.

And once you are away from your son or daughter, try to stay away. If the sitter has him or her out in the yard for the morning, do not keep appearing. If you have managed to get your child down for a nap, do not appear at the door (or window). The mere sight of you may start up unnecessary problems.

Because the child of this age can be so difficult with his mother, we strongly recommend nursery school attendance if possible and practical. Nursery school is ideal for this age when children like so very much to be with other children and to enjoy the multiple activities that a school situation can offer. This kind of relief, even three mornings a week, is quite enough for most Threes, and provides a wonderful respite for Mother. Somehow it seems to break into his tangled patterns of overdemanding.

Next, we recommend that you enjoy to their fullest those moments between routines when your child may be fun to be with. Enjoy your play with him since he will, if permitted, very much enjoy his play with you.

In fact, your very best technique, at this age or any

other, consists, if you can manage it, of establishing a good relationship between the two of you. Your child will do many things you want him to just because you are you. So, let him know you care. Let him know that you think he or she is just great—the best child ever.

You can, of course, do this in many ways. Physical expressions of affection work wonders. But beyond such expressions is the very sure support that comes from words. These do not have to be just words of praise. They can be about anything in the world. So, spend time with your child and *talk to him*.

(He on his part often wants to express his newfound

love for you. At Three the child "likes," but by Three-and-a-half he "loves." And he knows the difference. One Three-and-a-half-year-old boy told his teacher one day, "I love your hair." The teacher toned things down a bit and said she was happy that he liked her hair. His response was strong and clear. "No," he shouted, "I l-l-l-*love* your hair.")

Even at the relatively tender age of Three, your child will enjoy talking to you. His conversation may not be as fully fascinating as it may be when he is in his teens and you really want to know what is on his mind. But if you look forward to the prospect of good conversations later on, now is the time to start.

If your child is one who all of a sudden becomes quite unmanageable in stores or out on a visit, keep such occasions to a minimum. Four will love and will profit from excursions with you. Three-and-a-half may be better off at home.

If you are ingenious enough, some master plan can solve an entire problem area over a long period of time. Instead of enduring daily battles over some bit of the day's routine, try to find some big solution that will solve more than the immediate incident.

With her early waking and her strong demand for parental company, one little girl we knew was a daily disaster to her mother and father. They solved the problem by providing an early-morning "surprise" for her. If she played quietly and enjoyed her surprise without disturbing them, there would be another surprise next day. That took care of the early morning, with only the rest of the day to go. (Though, even here, this little girl showed her need for variety. After her parents had for quite a long time had extremely good luck with raisins and a few small cookies, she asked one day if they could not "vary the surprise.")

Remember that television can be your friend. Wisely used, it can keep a child happy, well behaved and out of difficulty for long periods.

If mealtimes are too difficult, and no baby-sitter is at

hand, you may find it easiest to provide as best you can and then tell your child, "There it is," and leave the room. Otherwise every bite may become a bone of contention.

Serious fights over dressing can be diminished by letting the child keep on his T-shirt overnight, and providing pajamas that button in the back. So, instead of having to get two garments off and on, night and morning, there will be few or no "over-the-head" problems. It will also help if as you dress him you can keep his mind off the fact that he is being dressed by talking about some future happy event.

Since emotions at this age tend to be rather fragile, a boy or girl may express many fears, especially fears of people of unusual appearance, of the dark, of animals. Within reason it is best to protect him, or at least support him when he is fearful. Do not be ruled by his fears, but do not, when they are at their height, force him to face the things he fears.

Any lack of wholeness may be especially frightening to a child of this age. "Broken" is an oft-used word. That is why "fix it" becomes so important. Toys should be chosen for their durability. And hopefully fathers will be willing to spend extra time, if need be, to make things whole again.

Any conspicuous physical disability, especially a broken limb in a cast, may be frightening to a child of this age. The cutting of a birthday cake, which destroys its wholeness, may produce an avalanche of tears and ruin a birthday party. Fortunately, his imagination often comes to his rescue, as when he bites into a cookie and thus destroys its round wholeness. He may then see the cookie as an elephant, a boat, and various other things with each succeeding bite.

Since the Three-and-a-half-year-old's fears, timidities, and anxieties obviously cause him great concern, try to make him feel comfortable about the things he fears or cannot do. If, briefly, he fears to go outdoors alone, go out with him. If he is afraid of heights or afraid to go down

the stairs alone, hold his hand. Or, make up little songs about the things he has trouble with—songs of a positive nature—and sing them to him in a friendly way. When he knows he is not alone with his insecurities and his inadequacies, he will feel a whole lot better.

Four will be a stronger, more secure age. Use this fact

in your talks with him. Help him to believe that *When he is Four* all these things that bother him (you can name each thing specifically) will no longer bother him *anymore*.

From Thirty months on into Three, many children, reverting briefly to babyhood, express a strong need to be carried when out on a walk. Knowing this, the wise mother or sitter will not undertake a walk without some means of homeward transportation—a stroller, wagon, or some other vehicle. A thirty-pound child isn't easy to carry. The stroller, which he may initially reject, can be used at the start of a walk to transport a doll, teddy bear, or other familiar stuffed animal. On the homeward journey, the child may need to be assured that his doll or teddy will happily share its place.

By Three-and-a-half, your walk problems may be different. The child may suddenly stop stock-still and refuse to budge. If walks give too much difficulty, your best technique may be to make a marked change in your child's day, and to stay at home for a while and build up new interests inside the house, especially in the kitchen. The activity related to the making of easy things like applesauce and gingerbread cookies, with their accompanying attractive smells to which he is increasingly sensitive, may relax his tension. And the time will soon come when he can enjoy a walk with you without turning it into a battle of wills.

Try to help him feel comfortable within himself that it is perfectly natural for a child of his age to stay indoors. You can make up a song about how when he was Two-and-a-half he loved to be outdoors and to walk on walls and curbstones, and how he knows that when he is Four he will want to be outside all the time. Now he is Three-and-a-half and loves to be with Mommy (or Daddy, as the case may be) in the kitchen learning to cook. But someday, you tell him, he might add to his song, "I'm going to surprise Mommy, put on my hat and coat all by myself, and say to her, 'How about a little walk?'"

Another possibility, if a walk gives trouble and, as so often happens, the Three-and-a-half-year-old refuses to proceed, is that an imaginative parent may successfully use some diverting technique. One mother, who knew that her son was coming into the Three-and-a-half- to Four-year-old's customary interest in garbage and garbagemen, left her balky child momentarily, returning with a wagon and trash can. She called out, "Garbageman coming! Any garbage today?"

And then, spying him, "How lucky. Just the garbage I need. In with you and off to the garbage dump." And so that he wouldn't take her too seriously, she whispered to him that the garbage dump was their own kitchen, where a cookie was waiting for him.

Fine motor coordination may now show a tremor. If your child's tremor and lack of coordination cause him difficulty, simply step in without comment and give the support and help he needs. Do *not* urge him to try harder or to hold his hand steadier. He is already doing the best he can.

If you are one whose child does enjoy an imaginary companion, you can sometimes encourage him to do things "nicely" in order to set a good example for his companion. If he is one who pretends he is a kitten or a dog, you may find that "Kitten" will quite willingly and graciously do things that your son John, habitually refuses. (But in this case you must remember that a kitten has a paw or a chicken a wing. If you want your child to respond to your requests—as in his bath—you had best say, "Come on now, give me your paw," or, "How about lifting your wing?")

Needless to say, if your child is still hanging onto his security blanket or still sucking his thumb, you will make the most of it. Anything that quiets him and makes him more docile and more comfortable should be fully exploited and appreciated.

As at Two-and-a-half, you will, if wise, continue to use

face-saving techniques. It is not essential at this time to prove that you are the child's master. It is more important that you and he or she get through the day in one piece, with nerves not too badly frazzled.

So, make heavy use of "How about———," "Let's———," "Maybe you could———." Use any phrase or any technique that will permit you and/or your child to withdraw gracefully from a situation in which he finds himself unable to comply with your command.

Remember to speak positively rather than negatively. Thus, say, "Let's put the books on the shelf," rather than, "Don't throw the books onto the floor."

And absolutely refuse to let yourself get mixed up in the preschooler's favorite game of "I don't love you." Just refuse to become emotionally tyrannized by his expressions of affection or disaffection. In his need to control his parent, the child of this age will use emotional threats *if* they work. See to it that they don't.

An interesting characteristic of the child of this age is that, at least in some, there tends to be a sudden building up of speed, a speed that may even get out of control and end in behavior that falls apart. Parents can often utilize this speed to organize and improve behavior. So the tentative, insecure, hand-holding child of Three-and-a-half, as he mounts the stairs, can be mobilized into an effective streak with the simple suggestion, "I'll race you upstairs."

But a parent should be warned that this same speed, if one is not careful, can build up until everything crashes and the child ends in tears. Limits must be set, even though it is sometimes hard to stop a child once he is embarked on a full crash course. A perceptive parent can sometimes step in and switch the child's interest before he reaches this stage. Or, a nursery school teacher will divert the activity of several members of a group before a communal block structure, for example, goes all to pieces and blocks fly this way and that. Such an episode may end up in hilarity, but all too often somebody gets hurt and tears result.

Distraction, which Dr. Colin Colew calls a "magic wand," is often your best bet with the sticky, stubborn child of this age. If you approach any situation head-on, you are likely to become locked in a life-and-death struggle. Distraction can resolve the issue before the battle is fully joined. So, if you see resistance setting in, talk about something else. Ask your child a question. Pay him a compliment. Tell him something interesting.

Or, make a sudden noise. Just clapping your hands together may do the trick. Or, turn on some music. Or, show him something attractive. Or, if things look really bad, produce a bit of his favorite food.

But even if you set limits, you may still have to deal with the persistence of the child who may test the limits to the extent that he even produces an explosion in you. This can be frightening, but children need to learn that parents, too, are human beings and that there are limits to their patience. (By Four, limits may be more easily set and more readily accepted.)

In thinking about techniques, it is important to keep in mind that some are virtually foolproof and will work with almost any child at almost any time. Others depend a great deal on timing, or on the child's age and individuality.

For example, with some the best possible technique is warning in advance. If prepared, they can stand almost anything. But there are some for whom warning in advance is the worst possible thing you can do. If warned in advance, they become nervous and apprehensive, so that not only does the warning not serve to smooth over the future situation, but it also spoils the present.

Most parents discover rather early whether their child is one who is helped and protected by an advance warning, or if he is one on whom you do best to spring things.

This brings up the question of whether if you are going out in the evening you should give advance warning and/ or say a formal good-bye. Of if you should just sneak out, dishonest as this may seem. Only trial-and-error will tell you what works best with your own special child.

Actually neither may work. Three-and-a-half-year-olds, along with their other fears, may express an almost hysterical fear of having their parents go out in the evening. Though no parent likes to be controlled by a child's demands, right while this special fear is at its height it may be kindest to keep evening absences at a minimum. This kind of anxiety is usually not long-lived.

In fact, whatever the anxieties and demands and frustrations of the Three-and-a-half-year-old, or of being the parent of a child of this age, try to keep in mind that this too will pass!

DISCIPLINE

This discussion of techniques attempts to convey our general attitude about discipline. Discipline, as most of you appreciate, is not the same thing as punishment. Discipline, rather, is a way of setting up the child's life situation in such a way that good, effective, desirable behavior becomes possible. Techniques themselves are one form of discipline.

As to your own *philosophy* of discipline, you may be an old-fashioned, authoritarian parent who expects your child to do what you tell him to, regardless, even when the demand may be unreasonable or beyond his ability. You may be a permissive parent who permits anything and allows the child to follow his own whim.

Or you may, as we recommend, follow a policy of what we call *informed permissiveness* or *flexible control*. That is, you try to fit your demands and expectations to things that it is possible for a child with the maturity level and personality of your own to perform. Knowing that your demands are reasonable, you make them firmly and consistently.

The more effectively you manage this, the better your discipline, the fewer will be the incidents of rebellion, disobedience, or "bad" behavior, and the less need there will be for punishment. (Though no parent succeeds entirely. There will in any family be some unhappy incidents.)

As to what kind of punishment you should use, if and when punishment becomes needed, this depends partly on your own temperament and partly on what works with your child. Temporary isolation works with some. Deprivation of privileges works with some. Some respond to scolding; others to more physical measures. An occasional spanking, if it works, is not immoral, though spanking should never be relied on as a chief form of punishment. (There is a certain type of strong-willed, prone-to-violence, mesomorphic boy who seems to need a spanking now and then. But a sensitive, slender, ectomorphic child could be very much upset by a spanking.)

The so-called behavior-modification people hold that you can get any child to do anything you want him to by praising the good and ignoring the bad. This kind of handling seems complicated or unnatural to some, but for those of you who would like to try it, we suggest that you read *For Love of Children*, by Roger W. McIntire.

Each of you will, of course, work out his or her own philosophy of discipline and methods of discipline, keeping in mind both your own temperament and that of your child. Most important of all, perhaps, is that, if possible, Mother and Father agree, if not about every detail at least about your basic approach. Two parents, working together, especially if they have a fairly good understanding of what it is reasonable to expect of their particular child, have a good chance of helping him to behave in a comfortable and effective manner, at least much of the time.

And when parents realize that any child, but especially one of this age, needs one parent's undivided attention for at least part of the day, you may find that many of the usual disciplinary problems simply do not arise.

THINGS TO AVOID

1. Try to avoid the feeling that your child should or ought always to behave "nicely," or that routines should always go smoothly if only you do the right thing. Espe-

cially at Three-and-a-half, there may be much daily conflict.

2. Don't feel guilty, or that you are passing the buck, if you leave a substantial amount of your child's care to a sitter, since many at this age do best with someone other than their own mother.

3. Even at this (relatively) late age, do not be unhappy if your child still sucks his thumb or cuddles his security blanket.

4. Do not conclude, just because your child may suddenly stumble and stutter, tremble and twitch, that something is necessarily wrong with him. Many boys and girls quite normally express great motor uncertainty, especially at Three-and-a-half.

5. Don't worry if your Three-year-old no longer sleeps at naptime. A mere "play nap" may give perfectly adequate relief to both mother and child.

6. Avoid correcting your child's speech, though if he puts a sentence together incorrectly, you can repeat it, using the correct form. And avoid trying too hard to help him get over stuttering or any infantile articulation. Enjoy each stage of his language growth no matter how immature.

7. Try to avoid feeling that your child is not eating as much as he should. Chances are that his own appetite may be his own best guide as to how much to eat. Try to avoid dampening or dimming his probably fairly good natural appetite by insisting on large quantities, or by pushing foods that may be especially disliked at the moment. One good meal a day is better than three bad ones.

8. Don't feel that you have a "bed-wetting problem" if your child still wets the bed at night, some nights, or even every night. Many quite normal children do not develop the ability to stay dry until they are Five or even Six years of age. (Pad them up good and tight to save on laundry, and don't make a fuss.)

9. Do not feel that you should be teaching your child

to read. Read to him all you can. Make books available. Let him see that you enjoy reading, yourself. And when the time comes, however early or late, that he starts picking out initial letters in books, or asks what does S T O P spell, by all means, respond. But don't push. Be sure that any interest in reading that may be shown is his and not simply your own.

10. Avoid any and all books that advise that it is up to you to "give your child a superior mind" or to increase his intelligence. It is not up to you to determine your child's intellectual level.

11. Avoid trying to "make over" your child's personality. Even at Three you will find that some children are easygoing, others tense. Some love outdoor activity and rough-and-tumble. Others are less athletic and quieter by nature. Some get on well with anybody; others will definitely restrict the number of other people, adults or children, with whom they relate.

12. And, finally, try to avoid any feeling that you must break your child's will. Strong-minded resistance is better overcome by gentleness and strategy than by a show of force.

chapter four
ACCOMPLISHMENTS
AND ABILITIES

Children vary tremendously in their accomplishments. There are the early talkers who already by Two have a tremendous vocabulary. There are others, equally intelligent, who, especially if they are boys, may not have much to say until they are Three or older. Remember that each child has his own timetable; each matures at his own rate and in his own way.

It is also important not to feel that you as a parent "ought" to be doing something special about your child's intellectual life. As Dr. Arnold Gesell wisely remarked, so long ago, "Mind manifests itself." The child's mind is not something separate from the rest of him. Rather, he demonstrates to us the state of his mind by almost everything he does. He walks, he runs, he climbs, he looks, he listens. He grabs a toy from another child. He cooperates with another child. He refuses to have his coat put on. He dresses himself. Or, he models clay, messes with finger-paints, builds with blocks.

All these things are examples of his mind in action. It is not necessary for him to learn letters and numbers, now or even when he is Four, to show you and others that his mind is in good working order. Try not to be self-conscious about your child's so-called *cognitive development*. This is just a term, vastly overused, that has come into the literature in recent years.

If your boy or girl has good potential, and if you provide a reasonably rich and lively environment and give him your personal love and attention, his mind will take care of itself.

So, we hope that even by Three or Three-and-a-half years of age your boy or girl will not have been pushed into tremendous academic achievement. And even though you should not be worrying too much about his so-called cognitive development, you may be interested in making a few checks as to whether his basic abilities are more or less in line with those of other children of his age. Here are a few things you may like to check for. Do not be alarmed if your own child is not a master of them all.

THE THREE-YEAR-OLD

GROSS MOTOR BEHAVIOR

By Three years of age, the child no longer looks, or acts, as topheavy as he did just earlier. Standing now requires little conscious effort. The child can easily maintain his equilibrium with his heels together. Most now exhibit gross motor sureness as they walk, can walk erect, and no longer seem to need to balance with their arms, but, rather, swing them freely as they walk or run.

Some, around Three, do walk rather knock-kneed, but this condition recedes rapidly during the following year or two. Shoulders are now held much more erect than earlier, and the protruding abdomen is much reduced. Normal walking is characterized by uniformity in length, width, and speed of step. Step is, predictably, longer than at Two.

Though stair climbing no longer remains the passionate interest it once was, the boy or girl can now alternate feet

going upstairs, even though not necessarily when going down. Three can jump from a bottom stair, can ride a tricycle skillfully, using the pedals. This is, in fact, the Age of the Tricycle. Most can, if invited, stand on one foot with momentary balance.

Three runs and plays games with abandon—mere locomotion is hardly a problem. But it *is* a joy. Thus, he gallops, jumps, walks, and runs to music, all for the sheer joy of it. He can get up from a squatting position without help, and can balance momentarily on his toes. In a nursery playground, the child likes to climb up inclined boards, likes to climb on the Jungle Gym, and loves to slide down a not-too-steep slide. Motor behavior, now relatively secure, can be a source of considerable pleasure to both girls and boys.

Postural control at Three is so well developed that the child can take walking and running steps on his toes, can walk a straight line, can walk backward. He can also catch a large ball with his arms extended forward stiffly, though he makes little or no adjustment of his arms in receiving the ball. He can throw without losing his balance.

The child is now more secure and skillful in a motor way than earlier, but he may actually cover less ground in any given period of time. Out for a walk, he now has more notion of a destination, and spends less time than he used to in walking on walls or in bumbling along byways.

In seven clocked minutes of nursery school play, we see a typical boy or girl stopping at no more than two or three centers of interest, with an accompanying decrease in back-and-forth movements around the room. That is, it is not at all unusual for a child to spend three or four minutes, or even considerably more, at one center of activity. Motor behavior for the sheer fun of motor behavior is still strong, but there is much less running around simply because attention span is short, than earlier. (*See* Figure 3.)

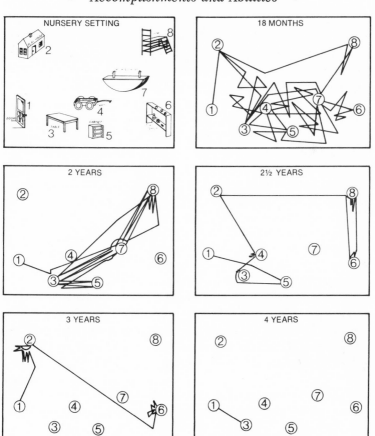

Figure 3
Seven Clocked Minutes of Nursery School
Behavior at Different Ages

VISUAL BEHAVIOR[1]

The typical Three-year-old is much more at ease in his visual world than he was just earlier. He can talk in greater detail about what he sees—what he experiences. He shifts his gaze to far-off objects and back to things close by, without getting lost or confused. People are more important to him now. He watches for changes in their facial expressions.

Hands now take a more directive role. They are used more independently of eyes. Block building is now carefully surveyed with the eyes. The child can look back and forth from model to product to judge how well he is doing.

Outdoors, Three takes a greater interest in landmarks than formerly, and is beginning to have a sense of direction. However, the boy or girl still associates special people he sees with special places. Thus, there may be confusion should the child meet his nursery school teacher in a store downtown. Or, as he rides in the family car, he may feel that other people driving in the same direction he is, are going to the same place he is.

The typical Three shows great interest in nursery school kinds of activities. He builds with blocks and makes simple clay models. He is "product" oriented. He enjoys looking through picture books, and boys, especially, are interested in pictures of machines, trucks, and fire engines. The child can talk about what he sees in books, though the less mature Three-year-olds have greater difficulty in combining language with seeing and may have less interest in looking at picture books.

The child of this age shows good facility in moving his eyes and can actually follow a moving target without losing his attention. His painting is now confined to the paper and doesn't spread to the floor or wall as it often does at Two-and-a-half years. Improved visual abilities help him to know where to stop.

Three can cooperate nicely with an eye examiner. His eyes coordinate well, and there should not be any signs of an eye turning. He can identify simple forms and with careful directions can respond to the tumbling E chart. Where there is any question of a so-called lazy eye, it certainly can and should be checked now, with a specialist.

Adaptive Behavior. A Three-year-old can do many things that require rather expert eye-hand coordination. He can build a tower of nine small blocks (though he may need to use both hands in steadying this tower) and can *imitate* a three-block bridge with two base blocks supporting a top block between them. (Six months later, his tower will go to ten, and he will be able to build a three-block bridge from a model, no longer needing to see it demonstrated.)

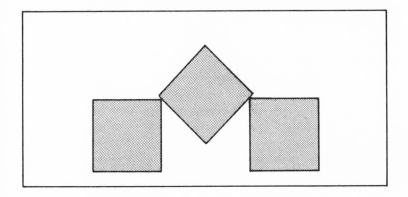

Figure 4

A Three-year-old can copy a circle from the drawing of a circle, and can imitate a cross if you show him how to make it. He may try to draw a person, though his product may not be recognizable as a person.

If asked to finish the Incomplete Man,[2] whereas at Two the average child merely scribbles on the printed figure and the Two-and-a-half-year-old adds only an arm or a leg, the Three-year-old typically adds four parts to the man, and the Three-and-a-half-year-old may add as many as five or six. (*See* Figure 5.)

The child is now quite adept at picking up small objects, readying his fingers for the grasp as his hand approaches

47

Figure 5
The Incomplete Man

the object. In writing with a crayon, he picks up the crayon by placing his thumb at the left of its shaft and his fingers at the right. He adjusts his crayon for writing with the aid of his free hand. He simulates adult grasp as he writes by resting the shaft of the crayon at the juncture of his thumb and index finger. Movements are still awkward, but he doesn't use his whole arm as much as earlier. Sometimes he picks things up with his nondominant hand and then transfers them to his dominant hand.

If asked to place three blocks (round, square, and triangular) into a formboard with holes of these three shapes, he can do so at once. And if the board is rotated, he can easily adapt to this, though he may make an initial error of trying a block in the wrong hole.

Hands are becoming so much more skillful in everyday activities that he can now feed himself with little spilling. And by using both hands he can pour water from a pitcher into a glass or cup, usually without spilling. He can also remove his pants in undressing, and can unbutton big buttons without popping them, though he still has great difficulty in buttoning. In lacing shoes, he often pulls out the lace as he withdraws his hand.

Play Behavior.[3] The Three-year-old, for all his improving fine motor behavior, that is, his increasing deftness with his fingers, still vastly enjoys gross motor play with *big objects*. He loves block play, especially play with *big* blocks. He loves to carry and tug and lift and combine these blocks into actual structures, which may be more elegant in what he calls them than in actual structure. He may combine his blocks with toy cars and trains to make roadways, garages, bridges. Or, blocks may be used imaginatively as coal, ashes, lumber. Or, he may use them just for climbing, so that he can be "King of the Mountain."

Like his earlier self, he also loves to fool around with sand—making cakes, pies, roads, tunnels. Or, he likes to make pies and cakes with mud and water, patting and smoothing his products into desired shapes. He enjoys both his products and the activity that produces them. *Any* water play is of high interest at this time. Children like blowing soap bubbles, "painting" with water, washing clothes, hanging them on the line, sailing boats, scrubbing, or just plain splashing. Clay, too, provides great fascination, and products are beginning to look like what he calls them and may no longer be merely round or fat blobs.

Threes love to combine things, not only large and small blocks but even more intricate things, such as Tinkertoys. With their increasing understanding of the relationship between parts and the whole, they enjoy putting together pieces of any total picture. Thus, working on puzzles is fun for them. They like the idea of "Does this piece fit?"

Fingerpaints may still be a better medium than real paints, but real paints, too, provide a great source of

interest. Strokes are more varied now and more rhythmical than earlier, and the beginnings of design are emerging. But the child may still be quite content merely to cover a whole page with a single color, with little effort at shape or structure. Most are quite possessive about their artwork and dislike sharing a paper, paint, or brush with anyone else. Each wants his own. Crayoned products, like other products, may now begin to resemble the things the child says he is making.

Doll play is becoming more imaginative. Children may no longer be satisfied with merely putting their dolls to bed and covering them up. Now domestic play may involve cooking for doll babies and feeding them, as well as putting them to bed. Tea parties are now popular. Or, any aspect of everyday life may be reenacted, with different children beginning to take different roles, even to that of the family dog and cat. In fact, dramatization and imagination are beginning to be so strong in some (they will be even more so in another six months) that to some extent they reduce the need for actual physical props.

Outdoor play, here as at any age, is enjoyed by nearly all, though the rough, active little boy will probably enjoy it more than the quiet little girl. Some Threes would willingly, if permitted, spend nearly all of the day outdoors, regardless of weather conditions. Others are more bothered by cold or damp.

Just an ordinary backyard, somehow, if equipped with even the minimum in the way of sliding or climbing equipment or places to dig, will fascinate for hours. Lucky the child who, in season, has the opportunity offered by beach or field or woodlot.

Books continue to be a major play interest of nearly all, and interest and attention span are increasing as they listen to stories. Children still prefer stories about everyday life, though interest now goes well beyond immediate home life. They like to read about the seashore, about a farm, about various modes of transportation, about what happens in the different seasons. They like stories about nature. They like stories about animals, domestic or otherwise.

Best of all (or worst of all from some parents' point of view), they like their stories read to them over and over again until they have practically memorized every word. Woe unto the parent who changes or skips a word or line. (And happy the child who, in spite of the easy access of books, has a parent who will tell him a continued bedtime story night after night.)

Alphabet books are beginning to be of interest, and some enjoy very simple riddles and guessing books. Now children are beginning to enjoy busier and more complex illustrations than the very simple ones favored at Two. Many children now like to look at books by themselves, and often like to "read" them to themselves or to others.

Music, as at most ages, can be a great joy. Though most will not sing alone, they usually will join in with others. They love their "own" records, and in groups like to gallop, jump, walk, or run in time to music. Some, however, prefer merely to watch; though if you listen very carefully you may later on find them practicing alone in their own room when they think no one is watching.

Play interest now involves the child's own possessions. He enjoys new clothes and likes to show them off. Some are beginning to share their toys. At least they hoard and hang onto them less than formerly. Most are even beginning to show a little interest in money and like to have pennies to put in the bank. However, so far, most have no concept of the cost of things, and play money may be quite as satisfactory to them as real.

Perhaps three-quarters of the Three-year-olds studied by us now watch television. Those who do not, for the most part, just don't have a television set available in their home.

Perhaps half still accept their parents' ideas as to what programs they should watch and how long they should view. Others decide for themselves (in extremely permissive households) or make a fuss, argue, and tease to watch more often or for longer periods than their parents think they should.

Most parents who do permit television watching, feel that it does add to the child's life. Programs watched most (1975) are "New Zoo Review," "Lassie," "Mr. Rogers' Neighborhood," "Captain Kangaroo," "Sesame Street," "The Flintstones." The cartoon form is favored.

LANGUAGE AND THOUGHT

This is an age when language is paramount. Vocabulary has now developed to the point where most children can have fun with language. They not only have most of the words they need, from a practical point of view, to express their thoughts, their needs, and their wants, but they have enough language so that they can begin to appreciate that words are fun. Now they approach and can be approached through words alone.

Most children now are very good talkers and can express all that they need to say. They use language to get what they want. Most are beginning to ask "how," "what," "why," and "when" questions. Most love new words and love to experiment and play with words, as in silly rhyming. The Two-and-a-half-year-old seemed to feel most secure with words he knew—the old and familiar. Three loves the new and unfamiliar.

He responds well to words like "new," "different," "big," "strong." "Let's make a different kind" can often induce a child to continue a situation in which he may be fatiguing. He can be persuaded to enjoy almost any activity if you tell him it is a "surprise." (The surprise does not have to be anything remarkable. Your labeling it a "surprise" is quite enough in most cases.) He adores the notion of a "secret."

Such verbs as "help," "might," "could," "guess what," "needs" are surefire motivators. And such adverbs as "maybe," "how about" give the child a feeling that he has a choice, and often induce compliance.

53

A Three-year-old may even do something he doesn't want to do if you can give him a good reason for doing it, such as, "Let's pick up the blocks so we'll have more room to dance."

Three-year-olds often refer to themselves as "I," no longer as "me." They can easily name pictures of things in their picture books and can tell what the people or things are doing. They know and can tell whether they are a boy or a girl. They can answer such questions as "What sleeps?," "What flies?," "What bites?" And most can answer one of two such questions as, "What must you do when you are hungry?," "What must you do when you are sleepy?"

They also have enough concept of space combined with an understanding of place words so that they can respond to directions to put a ball on or under a chair. And they can repeat three digits.

Language is, indeed, coming into its own!

LANGUAGE AND OTHERS

If a Three-year-old is in a social situation with both adult(s) and children, as at nursery school or in a neighborhood play group, he converses very freely. And, for the first time, his conversation is directed as much toward children as toward adults. (*See* Figure 2, page 14.)

Also for the first time, language is becoming truly reciprocal. Not only is the child interested in what he says to others, but he is extremely likely to reply when somebody else addresses him. (This was not always the case when he was younger.)

As earlier, the child of this age has quite a lot to say to himself. Language often seems to confirm his motor activity. "Go down like dis," he may say as he steers his tricycle down a grade. Or, "Now we go up dis way," or, "I'm climbin' up on this house."

Addressed to an adult, short sentences announce current, completed, or intended activity. Again, words confirm and support whatever the child is doing: "I'm going to make a worm," "This is a gawage. That's what I'm makin'—a gawage." Or, he reports what he *has* done: "I'm all fru with the blocks."

Very often, Three still asks for help: "I want you to go with me," "Me want a turn. Me just had a *little* turn," "Help me build my house right here." Or, in contrast, he may announce his own independent activity: "I'm older. I can put that up," or, "I can go by myself."

Similarly, he likes to express his own sense of being a big child: "Could a baby do this?," "She's a little girl. I'm a big boy," "I take my apron off by my own self."

Three likes to discuss his own imaginary play: "I'm a kitty, too, but I found my mittens," "I'm a gingerbread boy in a brown suit."

He asks for information: "Where did that girl go?" And gives information: "This is a skirt. Its name is skirt," "I used to sleep in a cradle because I was a little baby yet last year."

Or, a girl loves to talk about her parents and her home: "My daddy dressed me yesterday. He put on a clean dress."

A boy calls attention to his own products or prowess: "Look! I'm bouncing a ball." And he likes to comment about other children: "Look, Ann's made a nice house." Or, he may complain about others: "When I make a bubble he breaks it."

Much of a child's conversation with any adult is still self-initiated. He may respond to what grown-ups say to him, or, sometimes, he may not. The major advance over six months earlier is that children now talk to each other quite as much as they do to any adults in the picture. They not only talk to other children but they talk *with* them. Self-initiated commentary leads, but there is a substantial amount of response to what other children have said.

Self-initiated comments, which admittedly lead, include such as the following:

Statements of ownership, commands to leave property alone, or arguments about ownership: "Dat's mine. Get out of there," "Don't touch my cup and dishes."

Direct commands or name calling: "Don't throw things like that," "Naughty girl."

Aggressive threats are diminishing, and requests tend to be more polite than earlier: "O.K. You have it, and then it's my turn," "I need it. I'll give it back when I'm through. All right?" Or, a child may ask permission for an object or activity: "I want some blocks. May I have these?"

Excluding commands, so common later on, are just beginning: "Nobody else can come in here."

Imaginary play, which took place with the adult earlier, now goes on with other children: "Let's make b'leeve this is a boat," or, "Bow wow, I'm your doggie."

Or, conversation may accompany building play, housekeeping play, or any other twosome or threesome (or more) situation: "Michael, I wonder. I wish you'd come to my house sometime. I wish you'd bring your bike."

And, for the first time for some, the child shows his (clay) product to other children as well as to the adult: "See what I made. A huge one. Feel it, Fred, feel it. Feel it, Nancy, feel it."

Responsive conversation by no means equals spontaneous conversation as yet, but there is definitely some response to what other children have to say. A child may give the permission requested, or may make a reciprocal offer. He may repeat some fairly serious remark made by another child and then laugh as if at a joke. Or, as in housekeeping play, one child may start a conversation about some real or imaginary activity, and others may chime in, each with his or her own addition.

VARIANT BEHAVIOR

Language is now so strong and sure that the ordinary Three-year-old often may feel relatively little need to express anger or physical or emotional refusal of some request with which he does not wish to comply. Happily, even in the rather easily frustrated, temper tantrums decline.

In a standard examination situation,[4] which permits a fair comparison from child to child and from age to age, the child of Three, for the very first time, expresses refusal more in words alone than in any other way.

However, as Figure 6 shows, the Three-year-old is still not beyond sheer motor refusal of a difficult or disliked examination request. He may still, if he does not wish to cooperate, throw test materials or try to leave the table or the room.

Though his chief way of refusing is merely to say "No" or "I don't know," on occasion an examiner can bargain with him to do something he really does not want to do.

By Three-and-a-half, the preponderance of verbal over other ways of refusing is more conspicuous, and motor and emotional refusals have nearly dropped out. And the hallmark of Three-and-a-half is for the child to say "I can't" rather than "No" or "I don't know," as earlier. Or, he may say "I don't want to," or even "You do it."

THE THREE-AND-A-HALF-YEAR-OLD

MOTOR BEHAVIOR

The Three-year-old tends to be rather strong and secure and accomplished in his motor movements. Hands, arms, eyes, total body combine in admirable efficiency. Logically, one would anticipate that if the Three-year-old does well in a motor way, the Three-and-a-half-year-old should do even better, should be even more secure and strong.

But here comes one of nature's little surprises, an example of the kind of development that we have termed *interweaving*. As any child develops, in any aspect of his behavior there seem always to be two opposing strands or forces at work, and now one, now the other, appears to be dominant. So far as motor behavior in this age range is

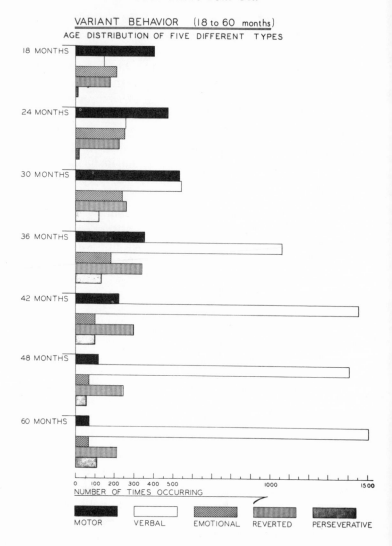

Figure 6

Age Distribution of Different Kinds of Variant Behavior, from Eighteen months to Five years

* Reverted behavior is appropriate behavior, but at a lower age level.

concerned, the two opposing factors that determine behavior may be thought of as coordinated security and uncoordinated insecurity. And at Three-and-a-half years of age, in many, the good, coordinated motor security often seen at Three breaks up.

The motor behavior of the Three-and-a-half-year-old, much of the time, may be described as insecure, uncoordinated, uncertain, tremulous, even helpless. There is, as it were, a stretching into new abilities with somewhat of a break in the middle. Thus, there is at this age much stumbling and falling. Lack of smooth interplay between flexor and extensor muscles results not only in the gross motor incoordination evidenced by stumbling and falling, but also by lack of coordination in the fine motor field as shown by a marked hand tremor in many children.

Some mothers feel that the child is "going to pieces" because his coordination is so poor. Thus, drawing products are now characterized by a thin, wavery line instead of by the earlier clear, bold strokes.

Speech, too, may be influenced by this temporary incoordination. The child may stumble and stutter. Visual difficulties are suggested by the frequent complaint, "I can't see," and by much twitching and blinking. Here again, the visual mechanism is stretching out into space at far and pulling further in at near, with the result that midspace becomes the breaking point. Tensional outlets increase. There may be not only eye blinking and stuttering, but increased nail biting, thumb sucking, nose picking, rubbing of genitals, chewing on clothes, excessive salivation, spitting, tics, and whining.

In fact, whining is a hallmark of Three-and-a-half, and can be extremely irritating. It may help the child if you can encourage him to express his inner feeling in a poem or song so that he may be in control of the whining instead of having the whining in control of him.

Emotional insecurity, which so many seem to feel at this age, may be based to a large extent on the temporary inadequacy of the motor system. Thus, the Three-and-a-half-year-old, in his insecurity and helplessness (which he feels, basically, in spite of his strong-minded behavior), may ask the adult to "Hold my hand," not only as he ascends the stairs but also as he descends. Even though a railing is there to support him, he still prefers the support of a holding hand.

Increased trembling of the hand, as well as a temporary difficulty with spatial orientation, means that many children who have earlier, without difficulty, been able to build a three-cube bridge, now have trouble getting the base cubes near enough together so that the third (top) cube will balance. Trouble with midspace may well be the cause of this kind of error.

Or, the child who, six months earlier, was easily able to build a steady tower of ten cubes, may have trouble in getting his tower to stay upright due to his trembling placement of the cubes.

It may be, in addition to motor ineptness, that the child of this age is trying too hard to perfect his fine motor control. Earlier he seemed to perform fine motor tasks easily and casually. Added growth obviously brings its own hazards.

In view of all this, it is not so important for a parent of a child of this age to know what specific motor abilities the child may be able to exhibit as to be warned that just because his own Three-and-a-half-year-old may suddenly stutter, stumble, blink, shake, and tremble, this is not necessarily a sign that anything is really *wrong* with him. Six months of added age should see him, once again, his old, nicely coordinated self!

And in spite of all this frequent ineptness and motor inadequacy, the Three-and-a-half-year-old much of the time shows himself increasingly skilled and effective in motor ways. Thus, he can jump rather high, rather far. He can go downstairs as well as up, one foot to a step. He runs smoothly and with pleasure. He balances nicely on a walking board.

He can hop on one foot and can hop in place on both

feet. Ball play is now effective enough that he may like to try catch-and-throw games. He can ride his tricycle without bumping into things, though one of his favorite games may be to crash into another child's tricycle on purpose.

VISUAL BEHAVIOR

The latter half of the third year is a transitional one, both developmentally and visually. The child is often over-aware and extremely sensitive. There is a kind of anxiety to his behavior, and he often says, "Don't look at me."

Coordination of fine and gross motor muscles as well

as coordination of the eyes is often faulty. It often shows poor timing. One eye may seem to turn inward periodically. Eye blinking as well as stuttering are common manifestations of motor difficulties. Building with blocks seems less facile as the child overestimates the space he needs between blocks. His structures are likely to tumble.

Visually there is greater interest in details, especially in the books he likes. Such an interest often brings complaints that he *can't see*, when actually the object in question may be directly in front of him. He puts all of himself into the pictures he looks at. He walks the path he sees in the picture, opens the door of the pictured house. Despite the poor timing of his movements he is movement conscious and understands that he can move without actually moving.

During a visual examination, the more mature Three-and-a-half-year-olds attend well to pictures projected on a screen. They can respond with considerable more certainty than earlier to the typical kinds of eye charts. When a doubling prism is introduced and the child is asked how many things he sees, he is able to report, "Two," a sure sign that he is seeing with both eyes simultaneously. This is a good time to confirm that there is nothing wrong with his vision—that the eye blinking and lack of visual coordination are a part of growth changes occurring at this age.

Those Threes who are progressing nicely on schedule are able to follow simple directions easily, can look without staring, keep their eyes on a moving target, are attentive to pictures in a storybook, and follow the story well. They also enjoy a wide variety of physical activities such as a slide or other types of climbing equipment, block building, ball play, and riding their tricycle.

ADAPTIVE AND PLAY BEHAVIOR

Though a Three-and-a-half-year-old is, inevitably, in many ways more skilled than his six-months-younger self, be-

cause of his increasing motor insecurity and instability some acts of skill are actually less well carried out now than just earlier. So, as noted, his bridge of three small cubes may not balance, his tower of ten may fall. However, there *are* definite advances. As much difficulty as he may have with balancing his bridge, he can now copy it from a model rather than, as earlier, needing to imi-

tate (that is, needing to see somebody else build it in order to show him how). And in play with his toys a child may show great skill.

He understands shape enough to be able to point correctly to six of the common geometric shapes. He feeds himself with even less spilling than at Three, and his pouring from a pitcher is now becoming rather skillful.

In completing on request the unfinished figure of a man (*see* Figure 5), he can now add a hand and foot to the earlier mere arm and leg. Eyes balance better than they did, though in drawing a spontaneous man most have not come very far, and the whole notion may still be beyond them.

Since hands do tremble, since children seem less secure manually than just earlier, or just later, Three-and-a-half is not an age conspicuous for advances in what we call fine motor coordinations and productions.

Play continues really not too different from what it was just six months earlier. The advance here seems to come chiefly in the increased complexity of interpersonal relations. Increased maturity seems to bring more an elaboration of and interest in other children than an increased ability to manipulate materials.

However, at this age the child can not only string beads but can arrange them by colors and shapes. Or, with a blunt needle and heavy thread, he or she can string macaroni to make "jewelry." But girl or boy still enjoys the simplicity of sand play.

LANGUAGE AND THOUGHT

Three-and-a-half, like Three, is a super time for language. Children will have more words when they are Four, but never again may words mean so much as in the Three-year-old period. This is because the sudden expansion in vocabulary, the ability to have fun with language, is now all so new.

The child of this age loves to play with language. He loves to make up new words. He adores silly rhyming. And he still responds beautifully to all those wonderful Three-year-old words: "surprise," "secret," "different." (Secrets are now most successfully imparted in a whisper.) It is fair to say that the Two-year-old acquires words, but the Three-year-old uses them.

Between Three and Four, language expands to the use

65

of different kinds of words and the beginning of correct grammatical usage. The child begins to use auxiliary verbs now: "would," "could," "be," "have," "can." Sentences grow longer. The child uses negatives effectively: "I don't want to go."

You can talk things over with him now (if he is in a receptive mood), and, as at Three, he will often do something he really doesn't want to do if you can give him a good reason. (In fact, when he is in the right mood, he can be a very reasonable little fellow.)

This is an ideal time for reading to the child. Many now enjoy listening to stories for as long as twenty minutes or more at a sitting. It will enhance any reading if you stop from time to time to ask the child questions about the stories or to allow him to comment or elaborate. At this age, children especially enjoy stories about anthropomorphized animals, such as in *Curious George*, by H. Rey. They also, with their interest in vocal extremes, love such books as Margaret Wise Brown's *Shhh! Bang!*

Children are now not only comfortable with language—they have words for the things they want to say—but they are discovering that language can be used as a tool for finding out things. They are beginning to ask questions: Why? How? What? When? Three-and-half to Four may be the all-time high for those interesting "why" questions. These, of course, even though sometimes trying, should be answered in full as long as you feel they are true requests for information. When they deteriorate to mere stalling—"Why do I have to?"—that is something else again.

According to Laurie and Joseph Braga,[5] in the age period between Three and Four years, children begin to use most of the sounds of their language fairly well. Most English-speaking American children use about 90 percent of the American English vowels during this time.

An increasing sense of space, combined with increasing command of the language, allows the child, on direction, to put a ball on, under, and beside a chair. He can now answer two comprehension questions: "What must you do when you are hungry?" and "What must you do when you are sleepy?"

By Three years of age, and increasingly at Three-and-a-half, not only is vocabulary increasing by leaps and bounds, but sentences increase in length and include both compound and complex structures. Tenses are beginning to be used accurately. Generalization is common.

And now the child easily integrates conversation and action. In fact, as noted, in some of his play imaginative conversation is so elaborate and satisfactory that almost any simple object (a block, for instance) can be anything he wants it to be.

How large is the child's vocabulary at this age? It is difficult to count, and we have no totally reliable figures. Some guess that the average Three-year-old may have somewhere around 1,000 words in his vocabulary; the Three-and-a-half-year-old, as many as 1,200.

The Three-year-old can, on the average, answer correctly eight of what we call "action-agent questions," that is, "What runs?," "What cries?," "What sleeps?," "What scratches?," etc. By Three-and-a-half, the average child can answer correctly twelve such questions. And most, by Three-and-a-half, know the names of and can identify correctly at least two colors. But parents should keep in mind that recognition of colors comes in at very different times in different children. Some girls know all their basic colors, including pink and lavender, by Three, whereas some boys even by Five may still have difficulty in distinguishing red and green.

From Three years on, you can teach children, if you wish, to play guessing games that will help them use language skills. They can guess about colors, sizes, shapes.

At Three, they may have been able to tell which is the big one and which is the little one of two objects. By Three-and-a-half, many can use such words as "best," "most," "biggest," "hardest" effectively.

Though many children, even at Three-and-a-half, express what are called "infantile articulations"—they especially say "dis" for "this," and "wide" for "ride,"— most by this age are comprehensible even to those outside the family. Some parents are unduly anxious about early mispronunciations, and fear that their child has a speech defect. If you are really anxious, it is wise to check with a speech specialist or speech clinic, though your very best bet may be to relax and wait. In the majority, early mispronunciations do drop out.

Another speech problem that tends to be exceedingly worrying to parents is early stuttering. Again, it may be calming to parents to know that it is a customary, usually quite normal stage that some children go through. In fact, in what we call a high-language child, that is, an early talker, stuttering may even come in at Two-and-a-half. Three-and-a-half, with its other motor uncertainties, is perhaps a more usual age for this behavior. Most speech specialists advise strongly not only that parents not worry about preschool stuttering, but that they not *do* anything about it.

The old-fashioned notion of telling the child to "slow down and say it over," or other similar admonition, is definitely not recommended. As a rule, the less attention you pay to early stuttering, the sooner it drops out. The thing you *can* do is to be sure that you give full and good attention to whatever it may be that your child is saying. This will reduce his need to talk fast and will reduce the likelihood that he will stutter.

The child of this age may express anxiety or discomfort by the very tone of his voice. When things are going well and he is enjoying himself, his voice can be loud and strong. But in a new or demanding or difficult situation, his high, whiny, tremulous voice bespeaks his discomfort. Or, when he is in trouble, his voice may become no more than a whisper.

Parents sometimes fear that their Three-and-a-half-year-old is deaf when he so often disregards what is being said to him. Surprisingly, he may respond best when whispered to. Actually, the child of this age may have many auditory *fears*. He is afraid of the banging of the radiator, the sound of a siren, the noise of thunder. He may even fear or be made uncomfortable by the sound of a loud voice.

LANGUAGE AND OTHERS

At this age there comes another major change in language directed to other people. The picture resembles that of six months earlier, but now there is only one leading kind of talk—*that directed by the child to other children.* He does talk to adults, and he definitely responds, when he feels like it, to what other children may say to him. But his conversation for the most part is directed to other children if they are present. And it is very varied.

Another change is that there is a great decrease in the amount of talk to self, accompanying solitary play. A child may repeat to himself something that has been said to him earlier: "Not safe enough. I'm not going way up there." But most of his solitary verbalization, even if not directed entirely to others, seems to have others in mind: "Here I come. Here I come," "I won't fall. I'm Five years old [not true]."

As just earlier, there is still a good deal of talk to any adult present (and some responding to adults), very much along the lines seen at Three years of age. There is no major or outstanding change here. Somewhat new, though, is the child's feeling of need to explain his own action in regard to some other child: "He would spoil it if I let him play." Or, a child may enjoy expressing his own moral superiority: "Not safe enough. *I'm* not going to climb it." Or, he may argue with an adult about some decision: "But we could both use it."

The chief conversation, in any group play, is thus, as at Three, directed to other children. It is fluent and varied. Statements of ownership, though they will diminish by

69

Four years of age, are still very strong: "My own ball. Get out," "That's *my* truck."

But—a real advance—children can now make "sharing" talk and suggestions for solutions instead of merely grabbing or commanding, as earlier: "Let me have yours, and you have mine. That would be a good thing," "You hold one side, and I'll hold the other." Or, a child himself may spontaneously suggest substitutions: "You could use that other one."

Or, engagingly, a child may ask permission or talk about turns: "May I step over your house?," "Pretty soon it will be my turn." Or, a child may use his imagination, and words, to lure others to play with him. Thus, Jim is playing his block "organ" in "church," but the other children ignore him. He calls, "Come on everybody, and sing in church."

Children use words to get other children to play with them, but, even more so, they use words to keep other children out. Excluding is a very strong behavior at Three-and-a-half, and it is enforced for the most part verbally: "You get out," "You can't play with us," "We don't want him in our house."

Imaginative play is strongly supported by verbalization: "I'm a monkey," "Come on, we're running an elevator here," "Michael, this is your office." This imaginative play can now be elaborate and long-continued, with much conversation. Thus, three girls in housekeeping play say: "We got everything we need?" "No, we need more berries." "O.K., I got blueberries and flowers. Let's make a cake." "Put it in the dish. Put it in the oven." Etc.

Doll play is highly verbal: "I have to go to the store. Will you hold my baby?" "Yes, I'll bathe her." "And then put on her new dress. Does it fit?" Etc.

And some of the girls are becoming quite interested in some of the boys (girls tend to be the aggressors at this age) and may say "Peekaboo" or "You sit by me now" or "This is just love pats."

VARIANT BEHAVIOR

The Three-and-a-half-year-old has many different ways of expressing refusal, and he uses all often. One of his best ways is just to stand stock-still and refuse to move or cooperate. Another is to use his good verbal abilities in a negative way: "I can't," "I won't," "I don't want to." Alas, he is by no means above just howling and screaming.

But in a controlled examination situation, in which it is possible for us to make reasonably objective and fair comparisons from age to age, he continues to progress in the direction of verbal refusals, which increase markedly. Other kinds of refusal continue to decrease. There are now twice as many verbal refusals as all other kinds (emotional, motor, perseverative) combined. (*See* Figure 6.)

This means that the usual Three-and-a-half-year-old, while being examined, can sit calmly at the examining table, and if he does not want to, or cannot, comply with an examiner's request, he merely verbalizes his intention not to do what is asked of him, without tears and without leaving the table, without throwing or banging or pushing or tearing materials.

chapter five
THE THREE-YEAR-OLD BIRTHDAY PARTY

The average Three-year-old is, at his best, a friendly, agreeable, sociable little person. Not yet ready for complex or prolonged social interchange, he nevertheless much enjoys play with his contemporaries.

Three enjoys the notion of a party, even though his actual idea of "party" may be rather vague and undemanding. A pleasant and brief opportunity to play at someone else's house, plenty of toys available, some simple refreshments, and a gift or favor for himself will in most cases satisfy him better than any attempt to have him take part in games.

Any group of Three-year-olds tends to vary tremendously in the social hardiness of its individual members. Mothers of more fragile—or wilder—children will need to accompany them on their social ventures at this age, standing ready to give support or to calm things down as the occasion may require. The length of time for which individual Three-year-olds can hold up socially also varies tremendously and should be kept in mind when the length of stay at a party is being planned. An especially shy or difficult child might, for example, come late to a party.

Most mothers recognize that many preschoolers are not at their best in a new social situation. For this reason they

do not consider it an adverse reflection on their upbring-
ing of their child if quarrels and difficulties do arise. They
simply and calmly separate children who are quarreling,
support any child who is not holding up. Parties do not
constitute an ideal situation for disciplining, so it is more
important to settle quarrels quickly than always to settle
them fairly. A difficult child should be removed from the
scene of the difficulty instead of being punished or
reproved on the spot.

KEY TO SUCCESS

The secret of success for a Three-year-old party is to
have the tempo very slow and the proceedings flexible
and unregimented. Three's expectations are not very high.
He is not particularly demanding of a party. Mothers of
extremely shy or boisterous children may need to stay
for the entire party. Other mothers don't need to stay; in
fact, their children may behave better without them.

Five or six children, both boys and girls, are quite
enough to invite. The number of adults needed to run
such a party are the host or hostess's mother and two or
three other mothers.

SCHEDULE

11:30–12:00   Arrival and informal play. A great deal
of the party at this age consists of opening, looking at, and playing most informally with the presents and with
the host's toys. Doors to the room where
the party table is set, and to any other
rooms that should not be entered, are
shut. Otherwise, guests are free to
wander at will.

Each child usually likes to bring a
present. Presents may be saved until all
arrive, then all opened at once. However, the time or manner of opening

presents doesn't really matter. Guests will be moderately interested in the present opening but are more interested in playing informally, especially in the playroom. Children play together some, but there is much solitary play. Mothers attend to children when necessary; otherwise, talk to each other.

12:00–12:30   Refreshment time. The table is already set up in another room. Use paper plates, paper cups, paper napkins. Have a piece of candy (gumdrop or marshmallow) at each place. Just before the children go to the table, the mother hands around a basket with little favors for each (cars, dolls)—preferably all of the same kind. Balloon decor.

Children sit around a coffee table in small chairs (some borrowed if necessary). Refreshments consist of very small sandwiches and milk. Some children may wander away but will come back for the cake, which is served after the sandwiches are finished. The cake is shown and the candles blown out. Then the cake is cut on the sideboard, and each child is given a *small* piece. Children will eat the ice cream but may pay little attention to the cake. Mothers, standing around to supervise the eating, may themselves like to eat simple refreshments—sandwiches and coffee.

12:30–1:00   Informal play. A second basket of party gifts, one for each child, is brought in. These gifts may be little dolls in baskets for the girls, airplanes or cars for the boys. (Or, if one prefers, some simple

74

toy appropriate for either sex may be given.) Children pick their own gifts— a ribbon on each gift allows it to be pulled out of the basket. Children then scatter around the living room or play-room. They sit on the floor with their gifts, rock on the rocking horse, play with puzzles or other toys, or with crayons.

1:00   Mothers who did not stay, return. All mothers gradually start getting outer clothing (if cold weather) onto children. The decorative balloons are taken down, and there is one (all blown up and tied with a string) for each child as he or she leaves. This final present helps them out of the door happily.

EXPENSES

This can be an extremely inexpensive party. The chief expenses are the ice cream, cake, favors, and one or two small presents for each child.

HINTS AND WARNINGS

It is most important not to try to make this party too formal. Don't try to play games. Remember that a Three-year-old party at its best is extremely relaxed and informal.

Be sure that there is a mother present for any shy or wild child. Have the mothers solve any problems that arise by separating the children involved—don't try to work out problems *fairly*. This is no time for discipline or for teaching moral lessons about sharing or about being a good host or a good guest. Remember that the host or host-ess does not have to accept too much from the guests just because they are guests. Remember that many children behave their worst at a party. Also remember that fre-quent presents help.

chapter six
HELP WITH ROUTINES

The Three-year-old in his daily routines, as in other aspects of living, tends for a while to be relatively easy to manage. His interest in the adult and his wish to please combine to make daily routines, in many, rather easy to handle, at least for the first half of this year. But as the child hits Three-and-a-half, his stubbornness, his need to do everything *his* way and not *your* way, often serve to make any and all of the usual routines less than pleasant for those responsible.

As one weary mother of a stubborn Three-and-a-half-year-old once confided, "I dread getting up every morning and thinking I have to get three meals into her before bedtime."

The problem is that many daily routines—getting the child dressed, fed, washed, and finally into bed—do, more or less, have to be carried out. The child knows this, and this is what gives him somewhat the upper hand. With many, rather skillful techniques will be needed if you are going to get him through his day with both of you all in one piece.

EATING

Appetite tends to be fairly good at Three. In fact, many Three-year-olds are described by their parents as good

76

eaters. For a while, around this age, preferences are less marked than they were earlier, and if parents are careful not to push, refusals may be few.

Meats, fruits, milk, and sweets are all on the preferred list. Vegetables are slowly being accepted, though if the child especially dislikes some particular type of vegetable, it is wisest not to push.

Most are reasonably skillful now in manipulating their

feeding utensils. The spoon is now grasped more between thumb and index finger than it was earlier. Some girls hold it adult-fashion, with the palm turned inward. Boys, however, are more likely to direct the palm downward, thus lifting their elbows, which can be a nuisance to someone sitting next to them on the side of the lifted elbow.

Filling the spoon is easily accomplished by pushing its point into the food and by pushing it inward. (The bowl of the spoon may be inserted either sideways or by its point.) There is good rotation at the wrist and little spilling. Some even like to use a fork, especially to pierce pieces of meat.

The cup is now held by the handle in adult fashion, and the child's free hand is no longer needed to help. The head still tilts back to secure the last drop, though in another year or two the hands can do the tilting.

Most Three-year-olds eat well alone in the kitchen, with their mother near at hand. Some can manage, without incident, at the family table. However, for some the family situation is too complex as they are likely to be too demanding of attention and their dawdling, poor table manners and food refusal are apt to get them into trouble, especially with Father.

It has always amazed us that families put up with mealtime struggles with the preschooler at the family table when a little planning to feed him before dinner would solve the problem so easily. If the preschooler does eat at the family table, he does best if he sits next to his mother, who can give him the attention he needs. And, hopefully, Father will refrain from lectures on table manners.

Unfortunately, as the child moves on to Three-and-a-half, mealtimes, even when the child eats alone, may become less harmonious. His arbitrary demand to have his own way about all routines may extend to mealtimes. He may not like the type or quantity of food served and may also object to the way it is served. For example, he wants his sandwich cut in two. But if you cut it vertically, it turns out that he wanted it cut horizontally. If you then cut it horizontally, that makes *four* pieces and he wanted only *two* pieces.

As with other routines, someone other than the mother may conduct mealtime more successfully than she. If it is going to be up to you, make every effort to avoid any contest of wills. Try to be, or at least appear to be, extremely relaxed about and even uninterested in the type of food eaten, *amount* of food eaten, and manner of eating.

Do what you can in advance to make things smooth by, within reason, providing kinds of food you know your child likes and, wherever possible, avoiding things he especially dislikes. Serve food attractively. If he wants to have the same food day after day, chances are it will do him no harm unless it is something to which he is allergic.

Keep servings very small. So far as you can, ignore poor manners. If you find that your child wants to argue with you at every turn, you may do best to put the food on the table, then tell him he can call you when he is finished, and *you* leave the room.

If, as some will, he absolutely refuses to eat, without making a fuss about it just let him know that another meal will be coming along in a matter of hours, and it is up to him.

Your child cannot fight with you about his eating if you absolutely refuse to be drawn into his arguments. If he can be made to appreciate that the whole matter is of only minimal interest to you, you will do best.

Though it is not within the scope of this book to discuss in any detail matters of either diet or health, nor do we wish to make any parent overly anxious about the kind of food his or her child may eat, we would like to give one warning. This is that some of the foods a child may like best may conceivably be very harmful to him.

Obviously, if they make him sick to his stomach, or make him break out in a rash, you will know it and will avoid such foods. But as physicians concerned about child behavior[6] are now pointing out to us, many foods harmful to the individual child may do no observable physical harm to him, but they *may* have a disastrous effect on his *behavior*.

Food or drink, or even things that are inhaled, may produce hidden allergies, which in turn can cause extremely deviant behavior. Thus, in some children dizziness, listlessness, fatigue, irritability, violence, and hyperactivity all can be induced, often by foods liked best.

And even without there being an actual allergic reaction, harmful food products, especially artificial colorings and flavorings, or junk foods (which, if possible, should be minimally available), have been shown to produce any or all of the above symptoms and, in school-age children, problems usually described as learning disabilities.

If your child seems to be happy and healthy, and if his behavior is reasonably satisfactory to you and to him, that is, if he or she is getting along all right in most respects, chances are you don't need to worry about all this. But if behavior is disappointing or unsatisfactory in major ways and you can't find the reason, at least consider the possibility that something in the child's diet may be at the root of his difficulties.

SLEEPING

Getting the child to bed usually becomes much easier as he or she moves on from Two-and-a-half into Three. Gone, for the most part, is the need for tedious and repetitive rituals that take so much time and patience on the part of the mother. Most are willing to get into bed and to release their parent after only a minimum of tucking in and loving.

If there is any objection and stalling, it can often be handled by the mother's closing her eyes and saying she won't look until the child is nicely under the covers. (At Two-and-a-half, she may have had to remove her whole person and shut the door.) However, as Three-and-a-half approaches, if the day's snags and tangles have put mother and child on very bad terms with each other, it may be that someone other than Mother may have better luck with the going-to-bed procedure.

Many Threes sleep nicely right through the night. Sleep troubles are in the past for some, but not for all. Interestingly enough, difficulty related to sleeping, if it occurs at all, tends now to come not at bedtime but in the middle of the night. Throughout this entire year many children do wake, get out of their crib, go to the bathroom, go downstairs, get food from the refrigerator, "read" a magazine in the living room, and may be found asleep on the couch in the morning.

Others—the more adventuresome—may even go out of the house if doors are not locked. A few may insist on getting into the parents' bed or at least on sleeping on the floor in their parents' room.

Since, as many parents have found to their sorrow, you cannot *force* a child to sleep, most find it easier on everybody to accept this nightwalking if and when it occurs. It works out well, with many, if you provide a night light that the child can turn on, easily available toys, or a little nonmessy food (for instance, raisins). If the child has trouble staying in his room, you can, if your conscience permits, tie his door loosely, since it is safer all around if he does stay inside his room. Then he can call out to you if and when he needs you.

As to allowing him to come into your room or bed, opinions differ. Your decision perhaps best rests on your understanding of your own child. If he or she is very flexible, and can give up habits and behaviors fairly easily, it may do no harm to permit it. If you have a child who tends to become fixed in a behavior once it starts, you're wiser not to fall into this trap. With many, if they are very insistent, it works well to put them to sleep in your bed but to tell them that when it gets to be your bedtime you will put them back in their own room. With an "easy" child, these middle-of-the-night problems can easily be solved. With a difficult one, you may have to use *much* ingenuity and patience.

Many Three-year-olds not only sleep right through the night but do not even need to be picked up for toileting. Others, if taken to the toilet when parents go to bed, will be dry in the morning, so the pickup seems well worthwhile. There is disagreement as to whether or not a child should be fully waked for this night toileting. We have found that sleep is less disturbed if the child is *not* fully wakened. If he is wet in the morning even if you pick him up when you go to bed, the pickup may not seem worthwhile, since some children are badly disturbed by it. Best then just to see that they are well diapered and in rubber pants.

Dreams are beginning to be reported but are not too disturbing in most, and relatively few children as yet experience night fears or night terrors. If a child does wake up crying, he can as a rule be rather easily comforted.

Most Three-year-olds wake rather early, often much earlier than their parents would prefer. Some can entertain themselves until it is time for the family to get up. Others may be impatient and disruptive. A "surprise," laid out either in their room or downstairs by the parents when they go to bed, can keep many children quiet until it is time for the family to get up. Food makes a good "surprise." The idea is, of course, that if the child is quiet and good, he will have another surprise the following morning. If he disturbs his parents, no surprise the following day.

Nap. A few may still sleep at naptime, but already, perhaps for the majority, the nap may be only a "play" nap. (At the other extreme are those who go on really sleeping at naptime right up into Five years of age.) Most are not too enthusiastic about this routine, but it provides a welcome and necessary respite for Mother from the child's company, and for the child from his own activity. Most, whether they like it or not, *will* stay in their rooms for the required time. If they are extremely active, and many are, books and/or toys should be provided to prevent the child from more or less wrecking his room.

In fact, the parent may do best to plan with the child

for this playtime. Special equipment or toys may be brought out just for this special time. And the presence of a timer assures the child that his play nap will end when the timer goes off.

ELIMINATION

Daytime wetting is a thing of the past for most. Even those children who have been slow to be toilet trained are usually dry, at least during the daytime, by the time they are Three. Those few boys who are not already dry by Three usually move into daytime dryness by Three-and-a-half.

Most manage this function very nicely now, with only slight, if any, help from Mother. Many "go" at routine times, with a fairly long span between, and few have "accidents" during the day. If on occasion an accident does occur, they usually insist on having their pants changed at once.

However, as the child becomes increasingly independent in his daily routines, verbal dependence on the adult may be the last thing to drop out. Thus, a child who may be quite nicely trained and seemingly able to manage this function by himself may still feel the need to tell his mother when he has to go to the bathroom. He may also, when finished, need to report what he has accomplished.

Most are consistently dry now after their naps, and many may actually be dry all through the night, with or without a night pickup. However (as later at Four and even Five), if the child does wet during the night, no fuss should be made. Merely pad him up tightly, put on rubber pants, and use a rubber sheet to save washing.

Some children do revert to daytime wetting when a new baby is added to the household. This should be accepted as a natural regression, and disciplinary action should definitely *not* be taken.

As for control of bowel movements, we find very marked sex differences in level of accomplishment. Most girls, by

83

Three, have this function well under control and have very few accidents or difficulties. Fortunately, the majority of boys have also settled down to a one-a-day routine and, like the girls, manage without difficulty.

But a surprisingly large number of boys are still not trained; in fact, may refuse to be trained. With some, this difficulty may result from sheer immaturity. They are just not "ready." But with others this lateness of training and inability or even refusal to function may be part of the life-and-death struggle that some are carrying on with their mothers.

For such boys, if your pediatrician's customary suggestions do not avail, we suggest the "newspaper-on-the-bathroom-floor" routine. Assuming that the child's time of functioning has more or less settled down to some one time of day but he still refuses to use the regular toilet and, instead, has his BM in his pants, there *is* something you can do. (If he has not yet settled down to some certain time of day, unfortunately you have a long, long way to go.)

At about the time of day when you think your boy may function, take-off his pants and underpants and let him play in the bathroom. Put an opened-up newspaper on the floor, preferably in one corner, and tell him that when he is ready he can "go" on the newspaper. We call this the "puppy-dog" stage. Part of the success of this technique is that children function most easily in a squatting position. A good many do respond to this suggestion within a week or two, and once the function has been regularized you can introduce a potty chair onto the scene and tell them they can use that.

Other boys use this particular function to control their mothers. Insisting that they cannot manage by themselves, they demand to be taken to the bathroom just when Mother is busiest or most occupied with other people. Even more exasperating are those who dirty their pants at such busy times and then insist on being cleaned up.

Some desperate parents, if the newspaper-on-the-floor

routine does not work, resort to forcing their child to wash out his own underpants. This may result in a reasonably well trained child in fairly short order, but we don't recommend it except as a last resort.

BATH AND DRESSING

The *bath* usually goes rather well; in fact, often rather pleasantly at this age. Some of the child's earlier bath rituals, having to do with shining the faucets or putting in or pulling out the plug just so, may still be present. But, for the most part, children now see the bath as a time to wash (or be washed) and enjoy it as such. Most like to wash themselves, at least the parts they can manage.

The only thing that most resist is getting out of the tub. If Mother will close her eyes and ask the child to surprise her, or at least tell her when he is out, this often seems to terminate a situation of which Mother, at least, has had enough.

For most, the bath is given just before bedtime and provides a relaxing prelude to going to bed. However, for some, especially at Three-and-a-half, the troubles of the day may have put both in a bad mood. On such days it does no harm if "just this once" Mother decides to skip the bath entirely. Obviously, this does no harm. Children, unless very dirty from play, don't need to be bathed all over every day. A little judicious hand washing and face washing and perhaps foot washing should, on occasion, suffice. The beach solves many problems.

Dressing, at Three, tends to go much more smoothly than at Two-and-a-half, when the child was very demanding about each and every ritual, and also better than it will at Three-and-a-half, when the child may object to *anything* his mother suggests. The Three-year-old is often much interested in what he can do to help get dressed, and undressing may be of even greater interest. Most are better at undressing than at dressing. In fact, most children at this age undress well and rather rapidly. Undressing is further facilitated by the newfound ability to unbutton front and side buttons, or an increased skill with zippers.

Dressing at Three includes putting on pants, socks, and shoes, and sometimes sweaters or dresses. However, most cannot consistently distinguish back from front, or button buttons, and though they may try to lace their shoes, it is usually not done correctly. Also, self-help in dressing depends a good deal on the child's mood. He may be very cooperative one day and uncooperative the next.

At Three-and-a-half, however, chances are that he will be more uncooperative than cooperative. Dressing is one of the many daily rituals that allow the child great opportunities for expressing the opposition to his mother's wishes that he seems to feel so strongly. Thus, every garment can produce resistance and an argument. Most Three-and-a-half-year-olds are more interested in resisting and objecting to the whole procedure than in showing their skill, as they may have wanted to do earlier.

Speed and a very firm tone are essential on the part of the person doing the dressing. Have his clothes ready and ignore his complaint that he doesn't want to wear *that* special garment. If he is willing and ready to put clothes on, permit it. Otherwise, you do the work. So far as possible avoid garments that need to go on or off over the head. Nightclothes that button in the back are thus essential.

As with other routines, almost anyone other than Mother may get best results.

TENSIONAL OUTLETS

A tensional outlet is not exactly a routine, but it is something that occurs all through the day and may well be discussed here along with eating, sleeping, and elimination.

Though your Three-year-old son or daughter may still be sucking a thumb or fingers and hanging onto a security blanket for dear life, Three, briefly, is a time when, for many, tensions diminish and many a child shows relatively little need of tensional release.

If your boy or girl *is* still sucking a thumb, and it worries you, be assured that nowadays most specialists seem to believe that it will do no major harm to tooth alignment (or to anything else) provided the sucking stops by the time the second teeth come in. If you yourself want to know how much longer it is going to last, do some checking. Chances are you may find that it occurs only part of the time now—perhaps when the child is hungry or tired or sleepy or frustrated, or just before he or she is going to bed. If this is the case, the behavior is probably on its way out. But if sucking still occurs much of the

88

time, and if at night when you remove your child's thumb from his mouth it comes out with a loud pop and goes right back in again, the whole behavior clearly has a long way to go before it will have run its course.

Three is in general a fairly relaxed time. Three-and-a-half is a different story. It is an age above all when the child feels tensions and often needs and uses many different modes of tensional release. This is an age of many and intense tensional outlets. Not only stuttering but eye blinking, nail biting, thumb sucking, nose picking, rubbing of genitals or masturbating, chewing at clothes or sheets, excessive salivation, spitting, tics, and simple compulsive patterns occur. The frequent whining that occurs at this age may also be considered a tensional outlet.

In addition to frequent eye blinking, Three-and-a-half-year-olds often seem to have other visual difficulties as well. Many complain that they cannot see. This complaint may represent a real difficulty in handling the intermediate visual zone, as children of this age when holding their own books often hold them very close to their eyes. At about this age or soon after, it is well to take your child for a routine visual examination to a visual specialist who is accustomed to working with children.[7]

chapter seven

THE CHILD'S MIND, OR HOW HE SEES THE WORLD

In the first year of life, a parent's chief interest in and excitement about his or her baby may be in watching that baby's increasing physical abilities. He first of all lifts his head, and then sits up, and then he crawls, and then he creeps, and then finally, wonder of wonders, he walks un-aided. Until the baby is talking, we sometimes think more about his body than about his mind.

But his mind is at work all through this first exciting year because body and mind are not two separate things. Your child demonstrates the working of his mind by almost everything he does. Even those first physical strug-gles and successes are controlled by his ever-active mind. They are by no means purely reflex actions. Your child doesn't have to *talk* or demonstrate reasoning powers to tell you that his mind is functioning.

And so it is in the other years of life. To observe, or to encourage, your child's mental processes, or to encourage the development of his mind, you do not need to concen-trate solely, at the preschool ages or at any others, on what he says, or on his ability to identify letters or spell out words or say the alphabet or count. You as parents *are* interested in your child's mind and in doing all you can to see that it develops to its fullest. But this doesn't mean that you have to concentrate on teaching him to read or

write or say his numbers. *You do not need to teach your preschooler to read.*

What you can and should do is see to it that he has as rich and rewarding an environment as possible. The most important thing in that environment will be you, his parents. And what you can do to help him the most is talk to him, play with him, read to him, listen to him, answer his questions.

You can take him on walks and simple excursions, letting him dawdle along the way, letting him walk on the tops of walls, letting him pick up twigs and stones, and talking together about the things you see.

You provide him, so far as you reasonably can, with a wealth of toys and play equipment. These toys don't need to be lavish, nor do they need to be billed as "educational" toys. Quite simple playthings, sturdily and safely fashioned, will do quite as well as anything more elaborate. Paint and fingerpaint and clay or Play-Doh will help the child develop his potential creative talent. Good strong outdoor climbing equipment (if space in your yard permits) will help develop motor skills.

Your child will give you needed clues as to where he or she is intellectually, what kinds of experiences and play equipment will suit him best at each stage of his development. His own "why" and "how" questions will tell you what he wants to know, and his interest or lack of interest will be your guide as to just how far you can go in your replies.

His language—the things he says—may be your best guide as to how far and in what way his mind is developing, but his actions and interests may tell you almost as much. You can tell what things really interest him by the way his eyes shine and by his persistence in returning to some special material or activity. You can tell when you have lost him by his restlessness and lack of interest.

A preschool child is an open book to those who take the trouble to read it. Watch your child and listen to him. He'll give you all the clues you need in your wish to provide a rich environment that will permit *him*, not *you*, to develop his mind.

Chapter 4 tells you some of the things you may expect your Three-year-old boy or girl to be *saying*. This chapter tells you some of the things you may expect of a Three-year-old as to his expected sense of time, sense of space, sense of number, sense of humor, and creativity.

SENSE OF TIME

Between Two-and-a-half and Three years of age, much that is new goes on in the young child's mind. *In no area does he advance more rapidly in this active period than in relation to his sense of time.*

More different new time words come in between Thirty and Thirty-six months than in any equal time period in the entire life span. The Two-year-old tends to live chiefly in the present, with small excursions into the past and future. But by Three years of age, most children refer rather accurately to events in the past, present, and future.

By Three years of age, most of the common basic time words are included in the child's vocabulary. Though there are still more different words for future than for past, there is nearly as much spontaneous talk about the past as about the future or present. And "yesterday" is used as often and as comfortably as "tomorrow."

The ordinary Three-year-old, though of course he cannot as yet tell time, does have words and phrases that refer to clock time: "what time?," "It's time," "this time," "I'm late," "in five minutes," "five o'clock." And he may make a pretense of telling time, looking at his watch and saying, "Past o'clock." Such phrases as "when it's time" can now be helpful in everyday living. Or, the child may ask, "Is it time for juice?" and may accept delay if told, "It's not time yet."

Words for the past may still be few: "last year," "yesterday," "other day," "other night." But words for the future are many: "tomorrow night," "next time," "sometime," "next year," "in three days," "tonight," "later on," "when he's older."

Not only is there much greater variety of future than of past words, but words for the past tend to be very specific: "last night," "last week," "last year." In contrast, future expressions may be more general: "later," "someday," "next time," suggesting greater maturity of notions of the future.

And, Threes can generalize: "every day," "spring," "a week," "every time," "all the time," "a long time," "some days," "my turn," even though accuracy of time expressions may still be at a minimum.

Children of this age like to use clock times, even though often quite incorrectly, in their play conversation. Thus, a child may pretend to telephone: "Hello, Daddy. It's about three o'clock. That's when you're supposed to come for me." Or, they may say, "Almost juice time," "Time for music," "When it's time."

The greatest increase in number of *different* time words comes in, in most, between Two-and-a-half and Three years of age. In the six months between Three and Three-and-a-half, there is not so much an increase in the *number* of time words used as in the *refinement* of their use. The Three-and-a-half-year-old child says such things as "It's almost time," "A nice long time." Or, he or she expresses habitual action with such a phrase as "on Fridays."

Children now are able to use many rather complicated expressions of duration, such as: "for a long time," "for two weeks." Or such phrases as "two things at once."

There are many different, and again rather compli-cated, ways of expressing sequence: "Bimeby I'm goin' to paint. Bimeby. We're not finished yet," "You see, I had it first," "Wait till Johnny gets through. Then you could have a ride, Mary." Or, "Just before we went to school, I saw a big scraper," "Before we put any toys in it we have to put a candle in and light it." Or, "I'm going to Sunday school tomorrow. Next day I'm going to play school."

Time games are enjoyed by some, involving your asking them what time they go to bed, get up, have their dinner, or what they will do tomorrow.

With increasing complexity of time expressions, in some there comes a confusion especially characteristic of this age. The child refers to future happenings as in the past. Thus: "I'm not going to take a nap yesterday."

Generalization of time concepts includes such phrases as "all night," "sometimes," "a whole week," "every year," "on Fridays."

Most can now answer, correctly, questions as to when they go to bed, have supper, get up. Most girls, though not all boys, can now give their correct age, though they may hold up three fingers in response to your question instead of responding in words.

One reason that time is hard for little children may be that they cannot see it—it is intangible and invisible. As Braga and Braga suggest, if you can translate it into something they can see, it may help. Thus, you might provide a big monthly calendar with spaces for the days, large enough so that you can draw small pictures in the sections. Each day, let the child cross off yesterday. Or, have a daily calendar, and each day let him tear off another leaf. Calendar work translates temporal order into spatial context—children can "see" that yesterday came before (or to the left of) today, and that tomorrow will come after (or to the right of) today.

SENSE OF SPACE

The largest increase in actual number of different space words takes place in most between the ages of Two and Two-and-a-half years of age. Most of these new words are still in use at Three, although a few of the more rigid and exact words or phrases, such as "right there," "right up there," etc., have dropped out as personality becomes more flexible with the coming of Three years of age.

A few new words come in now. Though not as exact as those used most at Two-and-a-half, they do express an increased refinement in space perception. New words include "back," "corner," "over," "from," "by," "up," "on top of," "downstairs," "where," "outside."

A new and marked interest in space detail and direction detail comes in at this age, particularly in answering questions. In telling how to get somewhere, the child may now give an actual direction: "Turn left and then turn right." (Such a direction may or may not be accurate.) In telling where his daddy is, the child no longer says merely, "At his office," but may spontaneously describe where the office is located.

The usual Three-year-old can tell you such things as where birds live, where fish live, where airplanes fly, where the roof is, where the chimney is, as he could just earlier. He can now for the first time tell you where buses go, and what is under the floor. (And by Three-and-a-half he can give you the name of the street he lives on, though usually not the number.)

He can now put a ball on and under (and by Three-and-a-half, beside) a chair, in addition to putting it on a table or giving it to his mother on command.

If asked where they sleep, most children by Three have narrowed down from an earlier "In my house" to "In my room." (And by Three-and-a-half, to "In my bed in my room.") By Three-and-a-half, most can also even elaborate on that and can tell that their room is "Near the bathroom" or "Near Mommy's and Daddy's room."

If asked where Mommy cooks dinner, most can go beyond the earlier general reply "At home" (characteristic of Two years of age) or "In the stove" (characteristic of Two-and-a-half), and can tell you that she cooks "In the kitchen." When asked, "Where is the stove?," the answer at Two-and-a-half is "At home"; at Three-and-a-half, "In the kitchen." When then asked, "Where is the kitchen?," the answer at Three is "Near ——"; and at Three and-a-half, "Next to ——."

If asked where they eat dinner, most have gone beyond the Two-year-old's "At home," and also beyond the Two-

and-a-half-year-old's "On the table." By Three, the child is likely to respond, "In the kitchen."

Thus, the trend is from the more general "home" to the more specific "In the kitchen" for both cooking and eating dinner.

If asked where he goes on his vacation, the child's answer at Three tends to be rather general, such as, "To the beach," narrowing down at Three-and-a-half to the more specific "To ——" (with some place name).

The further question "How do you get there?" is answered, at Three as at Two-and-a-half, by the name of a vehicle: "In the car." By Three to Three-and-a-half, the child may add, "Along such-and-such a street." By Three-and-a-half to Four, he may name places he goes by on his way. He may also actually be able to give a direction, such as "Turn left."

The very young girl or boy (Eighteen months to Two years of age) merely *looks* in the correct direction—as up or down—if he understands a space word. By Two-and-a-half to Three years of age, he may point if he understands the direction. By Three-and-a-half, there is little pointing and the child can use the appropriate word in context.

Concrete phrases such as "on the table," "in the box" are understood first. But by Three or Three-and-a-half, the child may be able to respond to the space words "on" or "in" without the addition of the place words "table" or "box."

By Three-and-a-half years of age, new areas of space are explored. The child now uses such words or phrases as "next to," "under," and "between," all of which show increased interest in appropriate places for objects. Interest in comparative size is indicated by "littlest," "bigger," "larger." "Way down," "way off," "way far" express expanding but also exact interest in location.

The child can now put a ball "on," "under," and "in back of" a chair. "In," "on," and "up in" are words much used. But most children are well on toward Three-and-a-half or even older before they can play a rudimentary game of hide-and-seek, really staying hidden as the rules require.

Children of this age are beginning to recognize like-nesses and differences in shapes and objects, and to be able to group things together, that is, to make simple classifications.

Individual Differences in Concepts of Time and Space. Though increasing maturity inevitably adds to each child's understanding of abstract concepts, by Three years of age we already find tremendous individual differences with regard to orientation in both time and space.

There are some children who very quickly develop good time and good space concepts and who even when very young seem to be rather well oriented in both. In other children, regardless of good "teaching," these concepts develop late and inadequately.

Some, of course, are well oriented in time but poorly oriented in space, or vice versa. But some are so poorly oriented in both that this lack of orientation may constitute a genuine handicap. These differences, for the most part, do not seem to be due merely to differences in intelligence. A child can be highly intelligent and still lack the usual level of orientation in either time or space.

SENSE OF NUMBER

Most Three-year-olds can count two objects and can even give "just one" or "just two" objects on request. Some are reportedly able to count to five, though it is more usual for them to count "one, two" and "a lot." The child's own activities may be influenced by numbers. Thus, he may demand "three" or "four" of everything if his concept goes that high, just as earlier, at Two-and-a-half, he wanted "one for each hand."

Number is beginning to be something that influences the child's own activity, and he seems to be becoming aware of the way things are related to one another in terms of number and amount.

SENSE OF HUMOR

Your Two-year-old may show occasional flashes of shy humor, but for the most part Two tends to be rather a sober little creature. Your Three-year-old will as a rule still be nowhere near as boisterously humorous as he will be in another year. (Four may report, factually, "I laughed till I cried.") But many Threes are beginning to show a certain sense of the humorous and even of the ridiculous. They laugh at others, and sometimes they can even laugh at themselves.

Two likes to laugh at incongruity or accident—he puts his mittens on his feet or his coat on inside out, or a friend bumps into something or perhaps falls down. Sheer gross motor accident or activity may seem very funny to him. Three's humor is becoming a little more subtle than it was, and definitely more verbal.

The Three-year-old's humor is also increasingly sociable. Two may have laughed chiefly at his own activity. Three shares his smiles and laughter with a friendly adult and likes to laugh at adult-initiated humor.

Humorous wrong guesses from the adult delight the Three-year-old. Such a simple wrong guess as "Are your socks purple?" (when actually they are red) seems exquisitely funny to him.

We see here the beginning of silly language, which for the next year or so will be such a delight. The child may say something as senseless as "Oozy doozy, oozy doozy," or "Squishy squashy, squishy squashy," "Golly wolly, golly wolly," or "Tickle ickle, tickle ickle." If the adult repeats this back to him, it seems even funnier. Or, he may pronounce a real word or phrase in a foolish way: "ho kog" for "hot dog."

Threes still enjoy accidents to themselves or to others, or simple incongruity of action, such as putting a ball on one's head, riding a bicycle in what they consider to be a funny way, falling around, walking on one's knees. But, increasingly, humor involves verbalization, and much of it may seem amusing even to the adult.

Thus, a child may call another by the wrong name, or tell him he is going to put him in jail. He may make up a story about a boat that climbed on a rock or a horse that bumped into an airplane. This sort of talk quickly moves into sheer nonsense: "The ham. The ham took the queen. The queen took the elephant. The elephant took the water."

Imaginary talk or play seems funny to the child who initiates it and to the child who hears it. Thus, a boy may say, "Have to give the fish some dessert," or he may ring an imaginary bell on his tricycle (which may be a real tricycle or may merely be made out of blocks and boards).

Threes themselves often use words that we adults associate with humor: "funny," "silly," "laughed."

By Three-and-a-half, the child laughs with or at an adult, shares his jokes with the adult, but now, increasingly, laughter is also shared with other children. In fact, now many laugh with other children more than with any grown-ups present.

There is still quite a lot of what seems to an adult mere silliness: clowning around and any wild way of walking or running or jumping, falling down, bumping into things, combining objects in an unrealistic manner.

Accidents still seem very funny to most, as well as any incongruity. Aggression (real or pretend) amuses many. Calling themselves or others by the wrong name always seems good for a laugh.

Typical kinds of Three-and-a-half-year-old humor include:

Incongruity. A boy or girl speaks in an incongruously deep voice, pushes a doll carriage crookedly on purpose, says, "My cracker's so good I want to spit it out," stuffs his own mouth too full.

Wild, Silly, Gross Motor Activity. A child may laugh and run wildly, may jump wildly, throw things around wildly, crash a truck down an incline.

Aggressivity. A child knocks down another's house, pushes another child down, kicks another child's train.

Silly Verbalization. Any words or phrases used in a fool-ish way delight. Thus, "ladada," "poopoopoo," "bumpy-boo," "Hello, Mr. Doo-Doo." Or, such a statement as "A house punched itself," "Lion got sick and a fish came and ate him up."

CREATIVITY: STORIES[8]

Probably your very best way of finding out what your preschooler is thinking and feeling is just to listen to him. Pay attention as he talks. Give him time to tell you the many interesting things that are on his mind.

A somewhat different but equally revealing approach can be to ask him to tell you a story. When he talks to you in ordinary conversation, he for the most part controls and regulates what he has to say. But when he tells you a story, he sometimes reveals rather more than he himself appreciates.

If it interests you to make this approach to boy or girl, you may find that Three is one of the easiest ages at which to obtain stories from children. Most Three-year-olds can express themselves rather easily in a verbal way. This, combined with the characteristically good-natured, coop-erative responsiveness of the child of this age to adult requests and demands, tends to yield enthusiastic, freely given, and often rather lengthy spontaneous stories. A minimum of blandishment and technique on the part of the adult is required to obtain these stories.

When your child does tell you a story, it may surprise you to discover what violent thoughts are lurking inside his head. Two-thirds of the girls of this age whom we have talked with, and more than three-quarters of the boys, include at least some violence in their stories. Harm to people comes first with girls, accidents second. With boys, accidents clearly lead. People falling down or things breaking are outstanding themes.

Most Three-year-olds, especially boys, seem to see their mother as a friendly, caring, and providing person, though some girls (no boys) see her as deserting them. All three-year-olds seem to see their fathers as friendly, caring, providing, or sympathizing.

Girls are the leading characters in stories by girls; boys, in stories by boys. Three-year-olds protect themselves in stories, mostly by having death or illness reversed or bad things fixed up. Another frequent protective device is to have bad things happen to animals rather than to people. Most children talk about things rather close to home. Realism still prevails.

Typical of stories told by Three-year-old girls is the following:

A horsie. He fell in the snow. He got stuck. And he bumped into a boy. He bumped into a airplane. The airplane broke. And then he broke a door. He broke a flying bird. He broke a boy. He broke a elephant. He broke into a book. Santa Claus came and brought him some presents. And some people came along and hit him.

Typical of boy stories:

Cowboys and Indians. They shot him. The cowboy shot the Indians. The Indians had to go to the hospital. Then they came out and shot the cowboys. And then the cowboys fell down. Then they had to be carried to the doctor. Then they got out of the hospital. Then they shot the Indians again. And that's the end of the story.

If the Three-year-old tells stories freely, one might expect that the Three-and-a-half-year-old would be even more glib and self-expressive. Not so. In fact, he tends to show considerable resistance. Children of this age resist not so much by actually refusing to tell a story as by arguing about whether they will sit or stand, stay near you or go to some different corner of the room, remain in the room where you are or go to some different room. Once all these decisions have been made, however, and they are finally cornered and settled, any storytelling tends to go smoothly and enthusiastically.

As just earlier, you may be surprised to see how much violence lurks, even if perhaps just below the surface, in your sometimes tractable Three-and-a-half-year-old. Two-thirds of the girls among the children we have talked to, and close to 90 percent of our boys, include at least some acts of violence or destruction in their stories. Of types of violence, in girls, harm to animals, aggression, and accident lead, in that order. In boys, harm to objects and outright aggression lead. As to kinds of accident, in girls, falling down is the chief kind. In boys, falling down and breaking something lead.

Kind and friendly themes are at a low point here, though food and eating are prominent.

Interestingly enough, there are extremely marked sex differences in children's attitudes toward their parents, as revealed in their stories. Nearly all girls see their mothers as friendly, but half the boys see mothers as punishers or as victims of violence. And while nearly all girls seem to think of their fathers as friendly, caring for them, sympathizing, or protecting, boys see them almost entirely as either deserting or ignoring or as themselves victims of violence.

(The difficulties so many teenage boys seem to experience in their relationships with their fathers apparently start very early in many, even though most preschool boys may not feel free to do much about their feelings.)

Girls, less violent and apparently less threatened by the adult than are boys, often give stories that are recitals of things that actually happen or might happen. (Interest in clothes comes in early in many.)

Typical of girl stories is the following:

Little girl fell. Went to school. Got a Band-aid after her nap. Went to school again. She buyed some glasses. Buyed a ring and a watch. Then she buyed some Kleenexes. She went outside to play and she read a book. Then she colored. Then she writed. Then she buyed some black shoes, some sneakers, and some blue sandals.

Boy stories, on the other hand, are much more violent. Breaking and destruction are leading themes:

A big cow and it broke. The cow broke down and broke my house down. Two of my houses. It broke the windows. It broke the Mommy of it. And then it broke the house down. And the baby monkey broke the pumpkin down. And it broke the big, big, big Mommy pumpkin down. Broke the girl down. A big, big, big light and it broke down. Broke the tree down and you know what? Broke the chestnut down on his head. Broke the apple down. Farmer with his brush and he bumped the car real hard on the head. Then he got his rifle. He shoot our car to pieces. He hit some boys off the car. And then another car came running over them. Both cars were running over me. Squashed me to pieces and then they sewed me up.

However, in spite of violence, as at Three a certain amount of self-protection is displayed. Girls protect themselves by having bad things happen mostly to animals rather than people. Boys protect themselves by having *objects* harmed, or by having death, illness, or accident reversed and things made right again.

CREATIVITY: IN GENERAL

Many of us (especially the noncreative) tend to think of creativity solely in terms of things that artists and writers and sculptors and musicians produce. Each of these areas of creativity can be approached, at least in a beginning way, by the child of Three.

He can tell (if not write) stories like the ones reported here. He can paint pictures with his paints or fingerpaints. Beginning sculpture is represented by the little figures he makes out of modeling clay. Even a not-too-creative child can enjoy himself in these media. And the very young child is also quite unselfconscious in his production of musical sounds. In fact, until somebody tells him otherwise, the child tends to be extremely spontaneous and also uncritical in his use of almost any creative material.

But there are countless other ways of being creative besides those we most frequently think of. Milton A. Young gives many good suggestions in his interesting book *Buttons Are to Push.*

He suggests, for instance, that you tell a story without an ending and ask your Three-year-old to make up an ending. Or, show him a picture and ask him to make up a story that this picture would fit. Either exercise calls for both creative imagination and logical reasoning.

Or, try asking your child to imagine a change in some part of his body—for instance, that he had four hands instead of two—and ask what he might then be able to do that he can't do now.

You can ask your child to look around for one minute and then close his eyes and tell you everything that he remembered seeing. Or, you could ask him to play the part of some object: a bicycle, bus, or eggbeater.

You might try blindfolding him and then have him try to identify various objects by their feel or taste or smell.

Growing a plant from seed involves a certain creativity and excitement. Taking care of small pets can also be creative. Even a walk in some new part of town can become a creative adventure.

Or, getting back to the more usual creative media, try drawing a few random lines on a page and then ask the child to make as many things from these lines as possible.

Everything is so new for the child of Three that he may not feel the constraint and self-doubt characteristic of many an adult when it comes to being creative. The very young child tends by nature to be highly creative and adventurous. With a little help and encouragement he may stay that way.

chapter eight
INDIVIDUALITY

There is probably nothing more interesting or more important to any parent than a clear understanding of his or her child's basic personality. So, it may seem surprising that except for the work of Dr. William Sheldon[9] there appears to be no thoroughly satisfactory systematic discussion of individuality that a parent can read.

Fortunately, almost every student of child behavior comes up eventually with at least a list of personality characteristics in which children differ. One of the best available is that of Dr. Stella Chess,[10] who suggests that we might usefully think of children in terms of activity level, regularity, adaptability to changes in routine, level of sensory threshold, positive or negative mood, intensity of response, distractibility, and persistency.

We are no exception to these list makers. Following are some important basic ways in which we have observed children to differ. The important thing about most of these is that they seem to us to result not from something that you as parents have done or have not done. Rather they are ways of experiencing and behaving that seem to a large extent to have been genetically determined.

Many of the ways in which your child behaves can indeed be modified. You do not have to sit passively by while a child expresses his inborn individuality. *But it cannot be ignored.* The more clearly you recognize your own child's basic personality characteristics, and the more fully you respect them, the more effective you will be in helping him to become the kind of person you want him to be.

It is a goal of many students of human behavior—a goal at present far from realization—that, first of all, parents might understand their own child's personality well enough to provide the ideal environment for him as he is growing up. And second, that the parents might help each growing child to understand his own individuality well enough so that, when he becomes an adult, he will understand himself.

For the most part we describe these personality characteristics that we have defined as opposite pairs. Your own child may, of course, for any given characteristic, be at either extreme or at any point in between.

To begin with, we have the *high-drive–high-energy* children and the *low-drive–low-energy* children. Diet, amount of sleep, chances or lack of chances for success— all may influence the amount of energy that any child expresses, but the basic differences appear to be inborn. Some individuals at Three or Eighty-three seem to have loads of energy, drive, ambition; others do not. High-drive children, in spite of all the energy they expend, seem sometimes never to get tired. Low-energy children, regardless of how little they do or accomplish, tire easily and quickly.

The high-energy child seems often to need very little stimulation or encouragement. He is most comfortable when active. The low-energy child, on the other hand, needs a great deal of stimulation from without. He needs to be encouraged to act.

The high-drive child seems always ready for anything. The low-drive child accepts only the tried and the true. He does not welcome the unfamiliar.

The low-drive child seems often to be fully satisfied with just one activity at a time, such as, for instance, listening to

music. The high-drive child, as often as not, is most comfortable when engaged in more than one thing at a time. He listens to music (or to a story) best if his hands are busy at the same time. This secondary activity does not distract him, as some fear it will; rather, it seems to help him to organize and attend.

A second important personality characteristic that differentiates individuals is the area of intensity of their concentration. At one extreme is the highly *focal* individual, who finds it easy and natural to narrow down and concentrate on a very small area, shutting out the periphery. At the other extreme is the *peripheral* individual, who finds it difficult to narrow down and concentrate, but instead responds at all times to many different, and often peripheral, stimuli. The focal child is not easily distracted by things going on around him. It is easy and natural for him to concentrate. The peripheral child is distracted by almost anything.

Though little has been written about the relationship of vision to personality, vision specialists have observed that often the myopic (nearsighted) person tends to be quite focal in response, whereas the hyperopic (farsighted) person tends to be more peripheral. It is important, in thinking about this relationship, to appreciate that the nearsighted person does not behave in a focal manner *just* because his vision is such that he sees most clearly things that are near to him. Rather, we believe that the social organism of this individual (not just his eyes) is geared to responding to things close by. And the same is true, though in reverse, for the farsighted child.

This relationship between one special part of the body (the eyes) and actual behavior is extremely important because it emphasizes the fact that though we do not know as much as we need to about the relationship between body and behavior, the probability is that to a very large extent *behavior is a function of structure*, and we behave as we do very largely because of the way our bodies are built.

Then there is the contrast between the *perseverative* child, who keeps on and on at the same thing, and the *child who tires very quickly* of any one task or situation. Though the focal child is not necessarily perseverative, it is quite usual for the focal individual to stick with a task even after its initial novelty has worn off. The peripheral person is often the one who cannot stick with things. He elaborates, creates, innovates, wants and needs to move on rather quickly to something new. The focal child is sometimes one who is happier to play inside the house; the peripheral child may greatly prefer the out-of-doors.

Another extremely important personality difference

exists between the *child who organizes from within*, whose drive seems to come from inside himself, and the *child who is chiefly influenced by the environment*, who must be not only motivated but also taught by those around him. That is, the extent to which children are dependent upon and responsive to the environment varies tremendously. The inner-driven child seems sometimes almost oblivious of things around him. He goes his way regardless. At the opposite extreme are those who seem almost completely dependent on their environment.

It has long been recognized that some people, children as well as adults, seem to be primarily influenced or controlled by their *intellect*; others by their *emotions*. It seems likely to many psychologists that the individual whose chief motivation comes from within may well be the more intellectual; he or she whose chief motivation comes from the environment may more likely be the one ruled by emotion.

(Among those who are more emotional than intellectual, there are, of course, also two extremes. There are those people who, though highly emotional, seem usually to have their emotions well under control. At the opposite extreme are those whose emotions rule them. Admittedly, with maturity, most of us do learn to control our emotions. Children are expected to be less well controlled than adults. But even among children there are those who seem to have pretty good control of their emotions, and those who clearly have very little control. They cry and scream around a good deal, are easily upset, prone to tantrums. They are hard to manage.)

Thus, allowing for all possible combinations of the above factors, we quite understandably have some children who, whatever their other characteristics, *adapt easily to the environment* and especially adapt easily even to a changing environment. There are others so demanding of the environment and so rigid in their demands that *the environment has to adapt to them*. And their demand even at Three (though less so than at Two-and-a-half) may

well be that the environment remain always the same. They do not adapt easily to change.

These children, the ones to whom the environment has to adapt, often seem to need not only a definitely structured environment, but may require, even as late as Three, much verbal affirmation from the adult: "Yes, that *is* your red car," "Yes, you did slide down the slide," "Yes, you did build that house all by yourself." Their opposites may be so independent that their own opinion and approval is all that matters. They need very little affirmation from you.

A possibly not very scientific dichotomy but one that almost any mother of several children knows is that of the child who is "not a bit of trouble for anyone" as contrasted to the child who during the preschool years is so extremely demanding that his mother literally can hardly get a bit of housework done because he demands almost constant attention. A subgroup among these latter is the accident-prone child who falls, tumbles, hurts himself, breaks everything in sight. In contrast, the no-trouble-at-all child, in addition to other delightful qualities, handles not only self but objects carefully and precisely.

Often he or she is also the one who, no matter how vigorous the activity, remains *spotless* in person and clothing. His more accident-prone counterpart, in addition to bashing himself up at any provocation, also tends to get very dirty and messy even when one would have said there was no dirt in sight.

Timing, or speed of movement, is another important matter of inborn personality contrast. Though many parents spend much time in trying to speed up their all-too-slow children (or, hard as it may be to believe, in trying to slow down their too-fast boys and girls), basic timing does seem to be inherited. Some children, from infancy on, *move very rapidly; others very slowly.* (And it is apparently not true, though some of the slow would like to believe it, that the slow-moving individual is necessarily more effective and accurate than he who moves more rapidly.)

114

Tempo and pattern over a period of time also vary from child to child. There are children who start slowly, or ineffectively, but then improve as a situation continues. That is, they have a slow, careful approach but consolidate and do better as they go along. Others, in contrast, start out with a bang and make a very good impression but tend to deteriorate as a situation continues.

Another interesting contrast in timing is the *time of day* when the person—child or adult—functions best. Though morality seems to favor those who get up early and go to bed early, actually most human organisms have their own time of day when they function most effectively.

Even quite young children can be divided into contrasting groups of morning children and afternoon (or, if permitted, evening) children. Some children wake up very slowly and do not show their liveliest behavior until late in the morning or even until after lunch or in the afternoon. Others (all too many) bounce out of bed at dawn and may be at their best and liveliest before their parents even have their eyes open.

And, speaking of timing, a further interesting contrast presents itself in childhood, and continues on into later life, between the *forward lookers* and the *backward lookers*. Some children are definitely forward lookers. They move rapidly and are always moving on toward the next thing. They complete any given activity quickly and seem always to be looking toward the next thing to do. In contrast, there are those who seem rooted in the present, or past, and find it difficult to complete any given task or situation in order to move on toward the next. Forward lookers often seem actually speedier in action than their opposites. (Children who live in the future are also the ones who can be helped by warnings or preparations for what may come next. They do better if prepared. Other children may become too tense and anxious if warned in advance and do much better if things are sprung on them.)

One kind of personality that, at least at its extremes, causes great difficulty and many problems for all con-

cerned, including himself, is the *perfectionist*. The true
perfectionist finds it difficult to try anything until he is
quite sure he can do it well, and thus finds it extremely
hard to try anything new. At the opposite extreme are
those who are willing to try anything, and are not at all
embarrassed or upset by failure or by a less than perfect
performance. Perfectionists, therefore, tend to be extremely conservative as opposed to their opposites, who
tend to be extremely adventurous. (One mother described
her oldest daughter as "my adventuresome eater.")

One further aspect of individuality, very important to
know about in understanding your own child though seldom discussed in books on child behavior, is the fact that
most children seem to have *some one area of their body,
or some one kind of behavior, that gives them the most
trouble.*

Thus, a child who is a poor eater may, if fatigued or ill
or if the world makes any overdemand on him, become
sick to his stomach. Another child, perhaps one who had
difficulty in toilet training, may have no trouble with feeding but may have toilet accidents if the world becomes
too much for him. And there are others whose sleeping
seems to be their most vulnerable area. Almost any illness or overdemand may interfere with their sleep.

All of these are only a few of the many different ways
in which you may like to think about your child. The
key to your own child's personality may lie in a realm
quite far from those we have discussed here.

One further aspect of personality difference that parents may usefully keep in mind is that though we can
predict that for most children "good" stages, or stages of
equilibrium, will alternate as the months go by with "bad"
stages, or stages of disequilibrium, we cannot predict just
how or to what extent your own child will express these
swings of behavior.

Some children seem always to be experiencing some
amount of disequilibrium, swinging over to the comfortable side of living only briefly. Others, fortunately, seem

to live, for the most part, very much on the comfortable side, their periods of disequilibrium being mild and brief. Life is a good deal easier for some children than for others.

The important thing, perhaps, is not that we should describe your particular child as that *you* should start looking for the keys or clues to his basic behavior patterns. Any adverse or difficult personality pattern loses its danger to some extent for both him and you if it is recognized. It not only loses its danger, but it can be exploited in helping to make life easy and comfortable for your child and for you.

So, if your child is one who needs warnings, you can warn him. If he needs structure, you can provide it. If he functions best in the afternoon, you can save difficult or demanding tasks or situations for this, his best time of day.

And the same applies to his strong points as well. You can take advantage of them and, perhaps, cease to fight them. For example, if your child is one who focalizes and likes to stick with one situation, you can permit him the time and opportunity to do just that, and not always try to rush him on to something else. If he is one who seems ruled by his emotions, you can approach him through emotion, and not waste time and energy appealing to his intellect, explaining and explaining to a child who is not interested in explanations.

In other words, your child's basic individuality or personality is strongly set by the body he inherits. But there is much you can do, once you understand this personality, to help bring out your child's strong points and to subdue his weak ones. Heredity always interacts with environment, and the environment can do a good deal to see to it that each child develops to the full extent of his potentialities.

Dr. Arnold Gesell, as long ago as 1940, emphasized the fact that heredity and environment inevitably *interact*. The words he used are rather long and scientific, but they are of such importance that we quote them here:

> In appraising growth characteristics we must not ignore environmental influences—siblings, parents, food, illness, trauma, education. But these must always be considered in relation to primary or constitutional factors, because the latter ultimately determine the degree and even the mode of reaction to so-called environment.
>
> The growth characteristics of the child are really the end-product expressions of an *interaction* between intrinsic and extrinsic determiners. Because the *interac-*

tion is the crux, the distinction between these two sets of determiners should not be too heavily drawn.[11]

SENSE OF SELF

There is an increasing concern nowadays about the child's sense of self—not as in the past simply about how he performs, but about *how he feels about himself.*

Clearly, two of the best ways to make a child feel good about himself are to let him know that you like him—that he pleases you—and to help see to it that for much of the time he encounters situations in which he can behave successfully.

The better you understand your child as a person, with all his strong points and his weak ones, the more effectively you can manage to see that much of the time he will be successful.

If he is totally unathletic, you will not demand too much of him along athletic lines, regardless of his age or your own personal persuasion. If he is shy and quiet, you will make him know that there is value in quietness, that not everyone must be highly social and outgoing. If he is somewhat slow of movement, avoid giving him the impression that speed is all that counts.

You can, and probably will, try to "improve" your child, at least in some respects. But try to do so without giving him the feeling that he is not a good and valuable person, as you know he is.

The young child to a very large extent gets his notion of what kind of person he is from the way he sees himself in your eyes. Your opinion counts. Let him know that it is a good one.

POSITION IN FAMILY

One aspect of individuality that some take seriously is the child's position in the family. There are those who believe that, in general, first children differ from middle or youngest children. Of those who hold this notion, some think that the differences are biological. Others believe that the differences exist because parents treat their different children differently. That is, they spend more time with their first child, pay less attention to their middle child, and baby the youngest.

If this concept of difference because of family position seems interesting to you, you might like to read *Birth Order and Life Roles*, by Lucille K. Forer, *or Family Constellation: Its Effect on Personality and Social Behavior*, by Walter Toman. Briefly, these are the differences usually described:

Firstborn children are most likely to become distinguished later on, and even as children they tend to be capable, strong-willed, effective. They tend to have a high sense of responsibility and a high need for achievement. They like to do things "right." They like to be leaders. Firstborn boys often are especially hard to raise. They like to have friends whom they can dominate.

Second or middle children tend to be less highly driven toward accomplishment, more spontaneous and easygoing, more tactful, adaptable, relaxed, patient. They are often more emotionally stable and better able to balance opposing forces than are firstborns. They are less likely, later on, to become eminent.

The youngest child, either because of his position or inborn temperament, may feel somewhat inadequate and inferior, may be more passive and submissive, more accepting of domination, more babyish, less driven toward accomplishment and excellence, more quiet and withdrawn than those born earlier. He, even more than the middle child, may develop indirect ways of getting what he wants. If he cannot get his way, he may either give in or turn to adults for support.

These descriptions are, of course, gross generalizations, and even if the basic theory holds, there could be all kinds of exceptions. A strong-willed middle child between two weak ones might be entirely different from a weak middle child between two strong ones. The sex of the child and the sex and also number of siblings would also make a difference.

Customary theories about the effect of position in the family on behavior tend to imply that it is what happens to the child after he is born, that is, how he is treated as a result of being the first, second, or other child in the family, that determines or at least strongly influences his behavior.

Those who believe that environment, or what happens to a child, largely determines behavior argue that parents are naturally inexperienced when they have their first baby and therefore have to practice, or learn, on him. They become more skilled and also more relaxed as they acquire more experience, and therefore do a better job on later children. There may be something to this notion, but we strongly question that this explanation is adequate to explain the great differences that often appear between first children and others in the family.

There is, however, another point of view, which we tend to favor. This is that a mother's body may actually need to "learn" how to reproduce, and that therefore there is a real physical reason behind the fact that first children, especially first boys, seem to have more difficulty in organizing their behavior and in behaving in an acceptable manner than later-born children. Often highly gifted, these first children also have much more difficulty in adjusting to life in an acceptable way than do later children in the family.

Along these same lines, scientists of this persuasion attribute special characteristics also to second and third children, based on biological reasons rather than on the way parents treat their children. Some, third children themselves, even talk about those "glorious thirds."

Whatever the reason or reasons that children behave as they do, parents often do like to observe and to think about the obvious behavior differences that do seem to occur rather consistently among first, middle, and later children in the family.

SEX DIFFERENCES

One further important aspect of individuality is the way any person interprets his or her sex role. Though many people nowadays feel that boys and girls behave differently from each other (when they do) largely because our society has *taught* them to do so, others cling to the more old-fashioned notion that very strong sex differences do exist from infancy on. Most nursery school teachers tend to be quite aware of the differences in behavior between the girls and the boys in their groups.

Though there certainly can be exceptions, boys, in general, in the early years seem somewhat less mature than girls. Even at the time of school entrance, many girls seem ready for the work of the usual kindergarten when they are Five years of age; most boys, not until six months later.

So here, at Three, you may expect girls to reach the querulous stage of Three-and-a-half a few months before boys may do so. But it isn't just a matter of timing, it is also a matter of interest. Young boys and girls do share many play interests, even to housekeeping play and dressing up. In fact, Three-year-old boys often dress up in skirts, shawls, and high-heeled shoes. But in housekeeping play, as a rule, boys prefer the role of father or grandfather or little boy, girls of mother or grandmother or little girl. And though both sexes may play with dolls, girls as a rule spend somewhat more time in a nursery school doll corner than do boys.

Boys seem to prefer gross motor activity—climbing, lugging boards around, building with blocks, or pushing their large- or small-wheeled vehicles. There is more rough-and-tumble play among boys—girls seldom push each other around or fall all over each other, and less often than boys do girls run and shout wildly.

Boys, being in general of a more muscular (mesomorphic) physique than girls, tend to be not only more aggressive but definitely more active in a grossly physical way. They seem, in general, more interested in dominating and in having their own way than are girls. They seem more interested in competition than girls do.

However, admittedly, not all boys are muscular, and some girls are. An extremely muscular girl can be virtually as active, aggressive, competitive, and domineering as any boy. And a boy whose body is rounder and softer may by nature be as gentle as any girl.

Boys undoubtedly learn rather early that some kinds of play, such as cops-and-robbers or wrestling, are more acceptable for boys, whereas doll play is generally considered more "suitable" for girls. And there is no question that children learn about their sexual identity, at least to some extent, by watching and copying adults around them. They see their mothers behaving in certain ways, their fathers in others. Little girls, in general, do tend to copy their mothers; and boys, their fathers. So that natural tendency is unquestionably reinforced by what they see.

However, it seems to us that the different book and story preferences expressed quite early by young children are perhaps *not* caused by society's customs. Though many good books can be shared by all, boys in general do show much more interest in stories about trucks, airplanes, and other vehicles and kinds of transportation than girls do. Girls from the beginning seem to prefer stories about people.

And quite marked sex differences are observed in the stories that children themselves tell. Girls at Three, as mentioned just earlier, tell more stories about girls; boys tell more about boys. Though both sexes tell stories of violence, those told by boys are much more likely to be violent than are those of girls. At Three, all children see their father in a friendly role; girls, only, see their mother as less than friendly. At Three-and-a-half, boys more than girls tend to see both parents as hostile or unfriendly.

124

For parents, it is important to be sure that you are not too rigid in the sexual stereotyping of your children. Try not to restrict them too rigidly by what you consider *suitable* for girls and for boys.

chapter nine
STORIES FROM REAL LIFE

MOTHER CAN'T STAND HER THREE-YEAR-OLD

Dear Doctors:

Please help me before I go out of my mind. My problem is that I can't stand my Three-year-old daughter. She drives me crazy. Always talking. Always moving around. Always wanting something. She has no respect for grown-ups, is constantly interrupting them.

She is especially obnoxious at bedtime. Keeps teasing to stay up a little longer, and then, when I give in and let her stay up an extra half hour, she doesn't appreciate it but teases for more. What can I do to make her better behaved? To add to the complexity of life, just four months ago I remarried. Marna does not have too good a relationship with my new husband and won't even mind him.

Ideally in high school (we judge that you may not be too far past high school age) you should have had at least a beginning course in child behavior. This would have helped you realize what young children are like. They are *not* miniature adults. They cannot be expected to behave like adults. They *do* keep talking, and they do keep moving around, they do interrupt, they do want many things.

One of the things they definitely do not want is to go to bed at what parents consider a "proper" bedtime.

To give you at least a notion of what small children are really like, you might try two of our own beginning books: *Child Behavior*, by Frances L. Ilg and Louise B. Ames, and *Infant and Child in the Culture of Today*, by Arnold Gesell, Frances L. Ilg, and Louise B. Ames. From these books, and from this present book, hopefully you will begin to appreciate that Marna is not out of the ordinary. She is behaving, from what you say, like a normal Three-year-old. There is not necessarily anything wrong with her.

You have a long way to go before you will be happy with your little daughter, or she with you.

ELAINE CLINGS TO HER MOTHER ALL DAY

Dear Doctors:

My problem is the extreme loneliness, and dependence, of my Three-year-old daughter Elaine. She has a puppy, but she ignores him. There are plenty of other children in the neighborhood, but she won't play with them. All she wants is me. For months now, from six in the morning until six at night (she won't nap), she follows me around. It is nerve-racking to say the least.

I spend at least an hour, morning and afternoon, exclusively playing with her. But twelve hours a day solid is just too much. I try so hard to be understanding as you say, but must admit that my nerves get pretty frazzled.

I can't even talk to another adult because she gets so jealous. And she gets terribly angry if Daddy kisses me in front of her. He is a Marine and not home too often. What can I do?

By Four, Elaine should have branched out, but of course you will be pretty well smothered before then. For the time being, you'll get furthest by respecting Elaine's de-

127

mands, within reason. Thus, have Father greet you with a wink instead of a kiss. Parents' kissing bothers many preschoolers.

And let Father greet her first and pay his first and most marked attentions to her. Since he is not at home much, this doesn't seem to be the biggest part of your problem.

What you must do, of course, is to start spreading her out, unsticking her from you and getting her, gradually, to accept other people. Choose her best time of day. Try, twice a week, to latch her onto a good, sympathetic, skillful high school girl baby-sitter.

Since these clinging children usually do better, with outsiders, out-of-doors rather than indoors, get her out-of-doors yourself and then somehow or other (you'll have to figure this out yourself) get away from her and leave her with the sitter.

It will soon be summer. Sometimes you can do this detaching act best at the beach where sand and water often capture the attention even of a clinging child like Elaine. Don't leave her alone too long at first, though.

Girls like Elaine do very badly in letting any outsider take over parts of their more personal life (feeding, dressing, going to the bathroom) but will often accept a sitter remarkably well for the plain stretches in between routines.

You may get some tears and wailing at first, but chances are she will eventually accept a sitter for increasingly long periods. Come fall, she should be ready for at least part-time nursery school. And if the teacher is skillful, separation from you should not be impossible after the first few weeks.

TRY TO GIVE IN GRACEFULLY TO YOUNG TYRANT'S
DEMANDS

Dear Doctors:

What *do* you do with a bossy Three-year-old? My daughter Sylvia is impossible. If she had her way, she would rule the entire family with a more than iron hand. "Do this." "Do that." "Don't do this." "Don't do that." "Come here." "Go there." "Now." And all the rest.

It seems to be her plan and intention to have complete control of all around her and to do nothing herself that her own impulse doesn't direct. What do you do with her? Give in? Talk her down? Let her have her way? Or make her realize that she cannot have her way? It is a real battle of wills all the time, and I am not sure who should win.

Perhaps nobody. Perhaps it shouldn't be a question of winning, though certainly there's nothing that the average Three-and-a-half-year-old enjoys more than a battle of wills.

The ordinary Two-and-a-half-year-old is very bossy, admittedly, but with him bossing is almost second nature and seems hardly to reach the level of consciousness. To the Three-and-a-half-year-old the battle is the thing, and when he meets his parents head-on, it is indeed a battle of wills.

Why this has to be, we aren't certain. It may be that in so many ways a child of this age feels insecure, that he has to prove his own strength and worth to himself by bossing all in sight.

Our advice is to give in gracefully where you can, and without even making an issue, when nothing is at stake, as in a play situation. You "do this," "do that," "put it here," etc., etc., as your young tyrant demands.

When there are things that must be done, don't make it a big clear and obvious point that you're giving directions and are determined to win. Rather, give commands in an offhand way and as if you were merely making suggestions: "Come on, now, we're going to do so-and-so," you say, walking away and not even waiting to see if she's complying. Chances are, if no face is to be lost, she will give in and "come along."

Battles will have to be joined sometimes in the course of a long preschool day, but the fewer joined battles, the better. You are undoubtedly bigger, physically stronger, and emotionally stronger than Sylvia. You presumably could beat her down, eventually, on almost every point. It is quite possible, though, that a child who was beaten down at *every* turn when Three-and-a-half might not bounce back with entire confidence, even at confident Four. She has to have her way sometimes. But let it be as easy and comfortable as possible. It isn't necessary for one of you to be defeated at every turn. Sometimes both can win.

JEALOUS BROTHER PESTERS BABY

Dear Doctors:

My problem is how to keep my Three-and-a-half-year-old-son Buzz from teasing his Nine-month-old baby sister. We thought we had spaced them quite well, but Buzz is apparently very jealous.

You have said that babies and preschoolers should be kept apart as much as possible, even if it requires a locked door. But now Baby is crawling all over the house, and it is difficult to keep them separated.

He loves to play with her, but it takes the form of, for instance, covering her up with a blanket as fast as she can get out of it, thus upsetting her and making it difficult for her to breathe.

I spend half my time saying, "Leave Baby alone." I have tried hard to ignore this behavior as attention-getting, but I am afraid it could result in her getting hurt.

It could indeed! Even though his attentions may seem primarily somewhat playful, Buzz could hurt his sister if allowed to play with her unwatched.

We urge you not to leave them alone together. This will take quite a bit of planning on your part and will be time-consuming, but it will be worth it.

To begin with, if Buzz is Three-and-a-half, hopefully at least part of the day he will be in the hands of a baby-sitter. Even if she is also sitting for your baby, she should be able to protect the baby.

Stagger naps if you can. When Buzz is asleep have Baby awake, and vice versa. If your baby is only Nine months old, she should accept a playpen for at least part of the day. This, hopefully, may protect her somewhat from her dangerous brother.

At any rate, it is not just a matter of protecting Baby when it is perfectly convenient. It is a matter of protecting Baby all day long, every day, until your son matures to the point that teasing, and possibly hurting, his baby sister has lost its fascination.

It is hard for most parents to appreciate the real hostility and even hatred that many small children feel for this creature who has come unasked into their lives and usurped so much of their parents' attention. No fun from their point of view, a baby is pretty much all to the bad.

Such directives as "Leave Baby alone" or "You ought to be ashamed of yourself, hurting your baby sister" are virtually valueless.

However, there is more to it than *just* protecting Baby from Brother. We have to think of Brother's feelings, too. Most mothers find that jealousy of the baby can be cut down considerably if Mother herself can spend extra time with a jealous preschooler. Also, if she can put effort into teaching him ways in which he can play with the baby safely and successfully, his violent and unacceptable impulses may be diminished.

EXPLAIN DEATH OF BABY SISTER AS SIMPLY AS POSSIBLE

Dear Doctors:

Three months ago my six-week-old-daughter died as a result of being a "blue baby." She died during the night, and when my little Three-year-old daughter woke in the morning, the baby and all her things were gone.

The doctor said she would forget in a couple of weeks. But I feel I have not given her a satisfactory explanation, as she still asks so many questions and pretends that the baby is still with us. She goes to Sunday school and has a slight understanding of God and Jesus. I know I will have to explain this question of dying to her again, as she has six grandmothers and five grandfathers of whom she is very fond.

Most of her Five-year-old friends have brothers or sisters, and she has been asking for a sister since she was Two. She is very old for her age in appearance and action. I have always explained things to her, but this has me confused. I never told her the baby was not normal, as she looked and acted like most babies. She was jealous of the baby only when I fed her, and helped me most of the time.

My husband feels it would not be fair to my daughter to have another baby until she is older. I feel we should have one soon to take the place of the one we lost.

You sound like a very brave mother. How *you* feel about all this should be a primary consideration here, not just how things might or might not affect your daughter. As to telling her, or, that is, explaining to her, about the baby, it is often difficult to explain death to a Three-year-old. But your daughter seems to have the perceptiveness of an older child. She has probably even now solved some of the problems in her own mind, since she goes to Sunday school and "knows" about God and Jesus.

It is best for you to explain things to her in your own way and in your own words. Very simply. Her own questions should be answered frankly and truthfully, but not in too much detail. And her own further questions, after you have answered the first ones, will be your clues as to how far to go.

But it is important to answer all questions she asks. (And be glad she asks them.) In the meantime, go ahead and plan naturally for another baby. This other baby may well be the best solution for both you and your little girl.

As to the grandparents, what you will in due time tell

her will depend on how old she is when they die. In general, even by Four years of age, the child's notions of death are extremely limited. As a rule, no particular emotion is related, though the child may verbalize some rudimentary notion that death is connected with sorrow or sadness.

By Five, in many, the concept becomes more detailed, accurate, and factual. Many recognize that death is "the end." (Though some think it is reversible.) Many do recognize the immobility of the dead. They may like to avoid dead things, such as birds or animals.

So, be realistic, be frank, be calm, and be truthful. Most very young children actually accept only as much of what you say as they are ready to absorb.

TELLING ABOUT ADOPTION

Dear Doctors:

I have put this off as long as I can. Our adopted son Timmy is now almost Four years old, and I haven't told him yet that he is adopted. Is he too young to receive this kind of information, and, if not, how should I tell him?

He is *not* too young to receive this kind of information, and the way to tell him is as simply and straightforwardly as you can.

Two of the things parents seem to find it hardest to tell children about are sex and adoption. The difficulty, we suppose, comes from their own emotional feelings about both subjects, since actually almost any parent knows the facts to be told about both, and is actually intellectually able to tell them.

Embarrassment or hesitancy in talking about adoption probably comes from two sources. First, the parent may actually wish that the child were her own and that the story did not have to be told. Second, she or he worries that the information may upset the child.

At any rate, most specialists agree that the time to tell about adoption is whenever the question or topic comes up. And if the subject doesn't come about naturally, then make the opportunity as early in the preschool years as possible. If you absolutely cannot think of what to say, you can get help from any of several good books on the subject.

There is a time-honored set by Florence Rondell and Ruth Michaels, called *The Adopted Family*, with one book for the parents and a second to be read *to* the child. A newer, and excellent, book called *And Now We Are a Family*, by Judith Meredith, gives basic information and also includes a good discussion of reasons why the biological parents were not able to keep their baby.

The basic facts you wish to convey are, of course, that you *chose* this child, even though you did not produce him, that you love him very much, that you are happy to have him in your family, and that his biological mother and father undoubtedly loved him, too, but that there were good reasons why they could not make a home for him.

Remember that, as in telling about sex, you don't have to tell everything you know or think about the subject all at once. And also remember that the more casual and calm you appear to be as you talk about adoption, the calmer and more secure the child will feel. He will be influenced by your *attitude* quite as much as by your actual words.

So, be early, be frank, be truthful, and be calm. But our advice is *not* to go overboard about the whole thing. Some people keep little scrapbooks labeled OUR OWN ADOPTED CHILD. Some introduce their child as "our little adopted son (or daughter)." Some even join groups of adoptive parents. In general, this kind of emphasis seems excessive and might suggest to the child that there is something very different about being adopted, and so may best be avoided.

BOY AFRAID OF TOY CLOWN

Dear Doctors:

I have a problem of fear in a usually fearless boy who is just Three. When he was about a year old we gave him a clown that rolls back and forth, with a very realistic face and eyes that roll. At first he seemed a little afraid of it, but soon he seemed happy enough. In fact, for a time he liked it so much that he carried it around.

A few evenings ago we saw a TV program about a circus. There was some violence in the picture. A knife thrower was trying to kill some other man, and although he wasn't dressed as a clown, there were clowns in the play.

I don't know if that caused it, but the next evening our son said, "The clown is going to hurt me." His daddy told him no, that the clown was just like any other dolly. This morning the first thing he said was something about the clown.

I thought about burning the clown before his eyes, but perhaps that would be too dramatic. We are going to leave soon for a vacation with his grandma. Would it be best to take the clown along or to leave it at home?

You seem to have made several mistakes. In the first place, the clown seems a somewhat dubious choice as a play object for a little boy. Second, a child of his age should not be watching knife throwing and other violence —people trying to kill other people—on television. We would definitely screen his TV viewing from now on. He is a sensitive child and appears to be extremely vulnerable to this kind of stimulation.

Burning the clown would indeed be too dramatic. It might lead to a fear of fires as well as a fear of clowns. We would most certainly not take the clown on your trip. Take some other favorite toy instead.

Since this special fear arose in relation to clowns and circuses, you might be on the lookout for a good circus book suitable for his age. A child needs initially to be protected from his fears, but then later he needs to experience things related to those fears so that he can eventually conquer them. However, this should be delayed until you think he is ready.

Your son's fear is similar to the fear of masks that children of this age often have. In fact, many Three-year-olds are afraid of any change of personality, and are also afraid of deformed people or of people who are a different color from the one they are used to.

FEARS OF THE DARK AND FEARS OF BEDTIME

Dear Doctors:

I am the mother of three girls. Their ages are Four-and-a-half, Three years, and Three weeks. My oldest daughter is going through a stage (I hope) where she is afraid of the dark. I go through a routine every night with her and with my Three-year-old. They always make the same requests when I put them to bed, such as not to let the bed go up in the sky or the moon break the house; not to let any alligators, cows, Indians, etc., into the house.

Is this just one of the many stages children go through? Or is this fear based on something done to them or something heard or seen? This has been going on for quite some time. It is becoming difficult to be patient with them. I would greatly appreciate any help you might give me.

As you suspect, fears like this are usually "just a stage," at least with most children. Though sometimes it does seem as if something that has happened or something that you have done may have set it off, usually the basic underlying cause seems to be deep within the child's personality.

That is to say, the same "frightening" incident could be experienced by several young children all at the same time, and perhaps only one of the group would respond with subsequent night terrors or bedtime fears.

How you handle the matter depends a good deal on the kind of child you have. With many, a rather fanciful treatment works best. Thus, you brush the bugs out of his bed, shoo the alligators away, exorcise the witches and ghosts, say a chant to the moon to stay up in the sky.

You give your child a flashlight to shine on anything that comes into the room after you leave. You provide a small, slightly glowing picture to hang on the wall and assure her (or him) that nothing can harm her as long as this picture shines. Since most of these youthful fears are fancy, fancy can often calm them down.

With other children, of a less fanciful turn of mind, you take an opposite tack and discuss and demonstrate so far as you can that the bed is empty of danger, as is the space under the bed, in the closet, behind the bureau.

Since a little more attention from you is what most of them are really after, whether they realize it or not, that little more attention, regardless of its specific nature, does the trick with a gratifying majority.

A story that sometimes helps is "Two Pairs of Eyes," in Crockett Johnson's book *Ellen's Lion*. This story tells of a little girl who overcame her fear of the dark by holding her toy lion over her shoulder so that she could look both ways. The lion tells her that his eyes are only buttons and that he can't see very well in the dark. "Nobody can," she reassures him, "but the [scary] things don't know that."

An important thing to check on is whether or not these bedtime fears change from week to week or month to month, or remain fixed and constant over a really long period of time. Like a tic or other tensional outlet, a fear that is fluid, fluctuating, and changing in its nature is usually a matter of less concern than one that remains fixed and unchanging.

ROCKING AND HEAD BANGING
ANNOYING BUT COMMON

Dear Doctors:

Sometimes well-meaning specialists aren't very serious about things we mothers consider to be most disturbing actions in our children.

Since cutting his first molar last fall, my Three-year-old boy has habitually banged his head on the headboard of his bed or even against the back of a chair if he is sitting up. It all started with the rocking back and forth of his crib. At that stage it was just a cute trick to us! We helped him by putting casters on the wheels! Later we moved him to a big bed so as to get our rest, as he was banging so loud that even our deep sleep was disturbed.

His banging against the side rail is enough to knock the bed apart and to cause the springs to fall to the floor. The complexity of keeping the child in bed, keeping the bed together, and keeping him from hurting himself doesn't daunt me as much as figuring out how best to help him cease this bad habit.

Your problem is a common one, but unfortunately one for which we know no guaranteed remedy. In a few rare children, sedatives do calm down their activity, though with others they make things worse. Thus, your specialist's response may not have meant lack of interest but merely that he, like most of us, didn't know how to stop your son from banging and rocking.

You put casters on the wheels of his crib to facilitate movement. As a rule, parents take the opposite approach —they remove casters and anchor the crib as much as possible on a thick, heavy rug. This sometimes slows things down, as the child gets less satisfaction from his motion. Of course padding everything in sight is the obvious and sometimes helpful move.

It is perhaps unfortunate that you have moved your boy to a big bed already. Usually it's best to delay this move until around Four—at which time the child is old enough to respond to such admonitions as "When you are Four and sleep in the big bed, you won't bang (rock, wet the bed, get out of bed, or whatever) anymore."

Our approach, if any, would be indirect. As with other tensional outlets, we would try to calm the child in other ways (make his day more satisfactory and less tension-producing) and at the same time give him opportunities in the daytime to blow off steam. Nursery school often works wonders in both these directions.

Often these rockers or head bangers have musical ability and interests, as well as high auditory sensitivity and awareness. They are often ritualists, with highly patterned behavior, and may be both slow in approach and slow in release. For this reason it is difficult for them to give up rocking and/or banging. Since Three-and-a-half is an age of extreme tension, these habits will probably not decrease in your boy during this period.

We have never known a child to injure his head from banging, and if your son bangs only on chairs and beds there is little likelihood of his doing himself damage. As to the rocking, try to think of things that will take the place of rocking in helping him go to sleep. Being read to, or just having you sit by his bed for a quiet talk, may help. Some mothers find that a good massage just before bedtime can relieve the child of the tensions that otherwise find an outlet in rocking.

Or, check to see if you put him to bed too early. Perhaps a later bedtime, plus pre-bed activity that would quiet him, might make the rocking (which, of course, is a release mechanism he uses to get to sleep) less necessary.

Some doctors find that both bed rocking and head banging occur most in hyperactive children. Some believe that this hyperactivity is caused or exaggerated by foods and drinks that are artificially colored or flavored. They report that a strict diet that excludes all synthetics does reduce various kinds of overactivity.

BE ENCOURAGED BY CHILD WHO SHOWS DECREASING
INTEREST IN HIS BLANKET

Dear Doctors:

My problem is with my Three-and-a-half-year-old son. Since he has been an infant, he has had a special blanket which he chews. I have never deprived him of it or made an issue of it because I could see no harm in it until recently. After he turned Three, I thought he should perhaps give up this habit. I talked with him about it, and sometimes while chewing he'll suddenly throw the blanket aside and say he's not going to chew anymore. This will last until bedtime, and then he'll want it again.

The last couple of months he has seemed to lose a little interest in it, only wanting it when sitting quietly or when going to bed. I can find no reason for this need of a blanket. He goes to nursery school every day and loves it. He gets along with his little brother and with his baby sister, so there is no jealousy problem.

Should I wait and let him discard it in his own time, or should I talk to him about it again?

You can be very much encouraged at the progress your son is making, His need for his blanket is obviously decreasing. More than that, he has accepted the notion that chewing his blanket isn't too good an idea, and he even makes voluntary efforts to discard it. Our guess is that another six months may see the end of the blanket without its ever having to become a major issue.

Some mothers find that a child of this age will accept having his blanket cut in two, or at least having a little piece cut off. With others, as you see their need of the blanket getting less, you can sometimes get it away from them for washing and then delay returning it or even forget to return it. With some, you can plan that when they are Four they won't need their blanket anymore.

With your son, since he is already doing so well, we would make no special issue except to comment favorably when he throws his blanket aside and says he's not going to chew anymore.

As to the "why" of blanket chewing, or thumb sucking, or any of these similar behaviors, parents often find it hard to discover any one specific cause. The tensions of growth itself are forces that the child needs to cope with constantly. Apparently some children feel tensions that can be relieved by blanket fondling or thumb sucking. These things seem to give comfort. If the child's personality and home environment are favorable, these needs and these tensions tend to diminish as he grows older.

TIMMY MAY BE SAYING "NO" TO SEVERAL THINGS AT ONCE

Dear Doctors:

My problem is that my Three-year-old son Timmy is not yet toilet trained, nor does he show any signs of readiness for training. My doctor doesn't seem to suggest anything I can do and I have tried everything—talking, pleading, shaming, spanking.

For the last few months I have stopped everything and just act as if diapering a Three-year-old were a normal procedure. This is fine except that it makes my husband very angry with both Timmy and me. He feels it is wrong to just do nothing. And he feels Timmy is old enough to be toilet trained.

Tim is a middle child—he has a baby brother and also a Four-year-old brother. He is a very lovable little boy, and we have a happy home except for the recent tension about his not being toilet trained. Why do you suppose Tim behaves this way?

Why does Timmy refuse to be toilet trained? Quite likely there may be real immaturity here. That is, Tim may not have been "ready" to be toilet trained quite as early as some others. However, since from what you say he seems quite normal, chances are that if all other factors were favorable, he could now be doing a bit better than he is.

When a Three-year-old still refuses to be toilet trained, we often suspect that he is rebelling (in one of the few ways he knows will be successful) against what he may interpret as too many pressures in other departments.

Three preschoolers in one family is not an abnormal

number, but it may seem like quite a crowd to Timmy. By remaining untrained, he is perhaps saying two things. First, that he would like to have a chance to be a baby for a little while longer. Second, that he wants and needs more attention from you. So, if baby-sitting arrangements permit, try to give him a little more of your undivided attention. Take him alone on his afternoon walk, for instance.

Actually his being untrained, though late, is not so dreadful except that it causes dissension between you and your husband. *He* is right, of course, in thinking that Three-year-olds are usually dry. *You* are right not to put pressure on and not to make a big fuss.

But this doesn't mean that you do nothing at all. Try treating Timmy as you would an Eighteen-monther or a Two-year-old. If, for instance, he wakes dry from his nap, get him to the toilet, and remark, mildly, on any successful functioning. Then find out what is his best and driest time of day and work on that, and continue to diaper him the rest of the day without comment.

More attention from you, and simple beginning efforts (without much fuss or talk) to take advantage of any dryness he may be showing should improve matters considerably, and soon.

TABLE MANNERS NOT SO GOOD

Dear Doctors:

My specific problem right now is that my Three-year-old son Ike has very poor table manners. About half the time he eats with his fingers. I feel that if I just remind him to eat with his fork, I am doing all I can.

My husband doesn't agree. He threatens to take Ike's plate away, and when Ike still doesn't use his fork, he does take it away. Then Ike cries and carries on, and everyone's dinner is ruined.

I don't feel that my son is learning anything in this

way, and I think all this commotion at dinnertime most every day is not only useless but harmful. How do you think we should handle this? I feel that a Three-year-old is too young to have good table manners. Am I right?

You *are* right. A Three-year-old *is* too young to have good table manners. Now and then some paragon shows up who seems to have been born using the proper fork at the proper time, but the average Three-year-old does well if he gets a reasonable amount of food into him without confusion. His method of handling spoon or fork, and other matters of manners, tends to be primitive.

You are right in not making a fuss about this. If you fuss, manners may improve slightly, but eating tends to go off. Getting a reasonable amount of food into the child is much more important than polishing up his manners. If manners are good by the time he is Five, you can consider yourself very lucky. Even as late as Six, many have terribly poor table manners.

Under the circumstances, the ideal solution might be to feed Ike at a side table while the family eats. Better yet, feed him ahead of time if his father will permit. One of the hardest things the mothers of many preschoolers have to deal with is not the child's immature behavior, but the father's unrealistic expectations.

If your husband continues to demand so much of Ike, and you can't change him, at least don't fight about it at the table. Children are more upset by dissension between their parents than by unreasonable demands that they behave better than they actually can.

SHOULD JANICE BE ALLOWED TO USE HER LEFT HAND?

Dear Doctors:

In another month our daughter Janice will be Three, and she is going to be left-handed, I'm afraid. She colors, writes, eats, unbuckles her shoes, play-irons, sweeps with her left hand. When I suggest she use her right, she does so, but quickly returns to use of her left. If I casually correct her, she says, "no, this hand" (meaning her left). I'd rather not make an issue of it, but since everything in this world seems geared to right-handers, I'd hate to have a frustrated youngster. Should I make a real effort to change her, or is it too late, anyway?

Is there any basis to the belief that left-handers see things backward, for instance, see the number 10 as 01, and that if you change them they are doomed to a mental crackup?

Don't try to "change" Janice. It is very important to allow any child to use the hand that he or she uses most easily and most naturally. (Particularly in a case like that of your daughter, who expresses so clearly her need to use her left hand.)

Even in the first few weeks of life, many children show a very marked preference for the right or left side, and this preference in many continues to express itself strongly throughout life. Though it is true that this is by and large a right-handed society, we still believe—and most other child specialists agree—that the child should be allowed to use his dominant hand, that is, the one that he naturally favors. Shifting hands does not lead to mental collapse, but it is not a good idea.

We doubt that left-handed babies as a rule "see things backward." Certainly, many children, when they start to read and write, go through a normal period when they reverse letters and numbers. Perhaps this occurs a little more in the left-handed child, but it also occurs in right-handers.

We hope that you will recognize that left-handedness is natural and right for your little daughter. Actually it seems to be so strong that whatever you do will probably have little effect on her. She will probably continue to be left-handed.

BOY, ALMOST FOUR, ANXIOUS ABOUT SEX ROLE

Dear Doctors:

My Three-and-a-half-year-old son Donald is giving me a lot of anxiety. The thing which bothers me so much is that he is constantly pulling on his penis and acting very foolishly.

His father is not living with us, and there are no other boys or men in the family. But I assure him that all boys have the same thing. He acts especially silly when I am bathing him and his Four-and-a-half-year-old sister.

Sometimes he talks about it, saying things like, "I don't want to have this. I want to be a *good* man." When he says this, I tell him it would be funny for a boy not to have one.

I am worried about this and don't know just what line to take.

Our advice would be not to take *any* special line. Just relax and be calm about the whole thing. Since bathing with his sister seems to bring on this type of conversation which you don't like, it might be best for a while to bathe them separately.

It is quite normal for boys of this age to be much interested in and somewhat concerned about their sex parts, their sex role, and all that goes with it. Tensional overflow at this time does seem to be in the genital region, and there tends to be quite a bit of handling of the penis. One mother commented recently, of her own Three-and-a-half-year-old, "He goes around hanging onto that thing as if it were a handle."

Another told us that sometimes when the family were driving along and the Three-and-a-half-year-old wanted to go to the bathroom, she would inadvertently ask him if he couldn't "hold it" for a while. She figured that perhaps he misunderstood and was taking her admonition too literally.

From what we know of the "old" days, it would seem that perhaps there was almost too little talk in the average household about sex. Now it seems that in some households there is almost too much talk and too much concern.

It is quite usual and normal for children around the age of Three or Three-and-a-half to be quite concerned about their own structure. Boys experiment with urinating while sitting down; girls try it standing up. Boys worry that they may lose their penises; girls sometimes worry that they don't have what their brothers have.

All of this should be accepted calmly by mothers and fathers, but not made a matter of concerned family conversation. It is, in most cases, a normal part of growing up.

NURSERY SCHOOL BENEFITS MOST PRESCHOOLERS

Dear Doctors:

My sister sends her Three-year-old to nursery school. The child loves it, and my sister says that every child should go to nursery school just as, ideally, every child should have a chance to go to kindergarten. Do you think this is true? It seems to me that there must be many children like my own who either don't need nursery school or wouldn't benefit by it.

By far the majority of children do, in our opinion, benefit considerably by nursery school attendance, even though they may have slight adjustment problems at the very beginning. There are a few notable exceptions, and your daughter may be one.

Thus, there are a few children so immature or dependent that the extreme and persistent difficulty of getting them to separate from their mother and adjust to the group makes attendance seem hardly worthwhile.

An occasional child is more than ordinarily susceptible physically and picks up illness after illness at school. Thus, school may be contraindicated.

For a few children, school attendance just seems to

take too much out of all the adults concerned. The whole business of getting them to school and adjusting them to school is too difficult.

And there are some children who get on so extremely well at home, whose play life, as far as playmates and equipment and parental supervision are concerned, is so smooth and rewarding, that it hardly seems that they need nursery school.

However, the advantages of nursery school are many. Among the many good things it can do for the child, especially the child of Three or Four, are the following:

It helps the child to learn to play with other children. It helps him learn to share, to take turns, to adapt to a group. It helps him learn how to get rid of aggressions in an acceptable manner.

It often provides physical play equipment, as well as toys, music, and art materials that the usual household cannot provide.

It exposes him to art, music, and story experiences sometimes broader than or different from the ones at home.

It provides a situation where he is less the center of attention than at home.

It gets him used to the idea of being away from his family, and gives him a life of his own.

If there is a home situation that bothers a child—a new baby or a too-competitive sibling—school gets him away from this situation and gives him a fresh outlook on life.

It gives him a chance to develop a close relationship with adults other than his parents or relatives.

It gives his mother a trained person with whom to discuss home problems of eating, sleeping, toilet training, discipline.

MOTHER BOASTS THAT HER THREE-YEAR-OLD CAN READ

Dear Doctors:
Recently you stated that you feel it is the imagination of parents if they think their Two-and-a-half- to

Three-year-old children can read. Would you believe that my son Dexter has been reading since he was just Three?

Our family doctor just cannot believe that Dexter has such a gift. What would you do with a child who can read any printing that is put in front of him?

I would be willing to have him come before any psychologist of your choice to prove to you that women of today treat their children like animals and that is why we are reaping such a poor crop. I, on the other hand, accept the responsibility of being a mother and participate in my son's activities and have taught him from the very beginning. Several nursery schools have told me that he knows as much as a first-grader. I will lay you odds you two will lose when you say a Three-year-old is not ready to read. All this is true, and I am not handing you a fictitious line.

You ask what you should do with a Three-year-old who can read any printing you put before him. Why, just keep him supplied with reading matter.

If Dexter can read like a child of Six, provide him with books you would give a Six-year-old. You may find that, as with many children, his relative superiority over others his own age may slow down a little as he grows older and the work gets harder.

This mother later replied politely:

When I wrote to you about a year ago, your reply gave me a perhaps deserved slap at my ego for boasting. I took it to heart and gave my views deeper thought.

Yes, I do have a precocious son, and, having time to devote to him, I was amazed and delighted with his ability to respond. It was at the height of this period that I wrote to you. Your letter was the sobering effect I needed.

The conclusion I came to was that it wasn't necessary for a little child to be pushed; just encouraged. My boy is a constant source of wonder to me, but so would any other reasonably bright child if given an equivalent amount of time.

I'm sure he could read for himself with a little teaching, but I have neglected this department of late.

The shift in this mother's attitude is very encouraging. We no longer fear for her son.

WHAT IS SPOILING?

Dear Doctors:

We hear a lot about the spoiled child, but my husband and I are not exactly sure what this means. Will you give us your definition of spoiling?

Some parents fear that if they give in to a child in any way, if they make things easy for him or let him have the things he wants or do the things he wants to do, he will be spoiled. Others believe that if they show affection, if they praise, if they give their child a good opinion of himself, they will spoil him.

All of these things are perfectly safe to do, within reason. In fact, in our experience the parent who is alert to the danger of spoiling is seldom the one who spoils.

The parents who bring up the most spoiled children are seldom aware that they are spoiling, and in fact apparently seldom give any thought to the whole subject. They are often somewhat undisciplined individuals themselves.

Well, all right, what *do* we think spoiling consists of?

It is chiefly this: giving in to a child, or reversing your command or direction or refusal, simply because he howls or objects or resists or refuses to obey you. You say, "No, you cannot go over to Georgie's," or, "No, you can't have any more candy." And then he cries or she fusses and you give in and say, "Oh, all right." That's spoiling.

For gradually the child learns that he can get his own way simply by refusing to take "No" for an answer. And thus he will soon manage to get his own way, right or wrong, all the time. This is the spoiled child.

But for a parent to moderate his demands in the first place, because he or she realizes that a child is strong-willed or immature, or on some particular occasion is desperately anxious to do something or not do something special—that, usually, is not spoiling.

EPILOGUE

The typical Three-year-old boy or girl has experienced a great deal of growing up in those months between his third and fourth birthday. He has experienced wild swings of behavior. He has progressed from a time when he was, as a rule, comfortable, friendly, gentle, cooperative, and reasonably secure in himself and in his relations with others, to a time of tremendous insecurity.

The Three-year-old, as we have pointed out, tends to be a person who enjoys life and whom others enjoy. The Three-and-a-half-year-old is often one who finds difficulty in nearly everything he does. Life for him is beset by threats and dangers, fears and anxieties.

Happily, for most, once the fourth birthday arrives, insecurity and withdrawal become things of the past. The typical Four-year-old is a person of vast exuberance, tremendous enthusiasm, beautiful self-confidence. He is one who loves life so very much that he can "hardly wait" for each of the wonderful things that make up his day and his living.

And for parents, Four is in most cases an age well worth waiting for.

APPENDIXES
Good Toys
for Three-Year-Olds

Balls
Baskets and boxes
Beanbags
Block-printing equipment
Blocks
Blunt scissors
Boards and sawhorse for seesaw
Boards for balancing and sliding
Books
Bouncing board
Braided strings with rigid tips for stringing beads
Brushes for painting
Cards with holes punched in them
Chest of drawers, cupboard
Clay
Climbing apparatus such as Jungle Gym, Tower Gym, ladders, boxes
Cloth books with pages for lacing
Color and shape and design materials, such as bits of plastic or felt that adhere to a larger picture surface, or pregummed paper mosaic pieces
Colored construction paper
Costume box, including pocketbooks, hats, gloves, scarves, jewelry, curtains
Crayons, large-size
Dishes and cooking utensils
Doll bed, carriage, high chair
Doll clothing with large buttons and buttonholes
Dolls
Doorway gym
Easel
Easel paper
Felt pens
Hand puppets
Hollow blocks
Housekeeping toys (carpet sweeper, broom, dust mop)
Interlocking block trains
Kegs
Large beads to string
Laundry tub, ironing board, iron, adult-size clothespins
Logs

Materials for playing house, store, train

Musical instruments, such as wrist bells, drum, tambourine, castanets, triangle

Nature specimens, such as fish, turtles, salamanders, rabbits, guinea pigs, or plants (These, of course, are not really toys.)

Nests of boxes or cans

Packing boxes, large and sturdy enough for child to climb on

Paints

Phonograph and records

Poster paints, fingerpaints, easel

Puzzles

Rocking horse

Rope and string

Sand toys, including spoon, sugar scoop, pail, cans, sifter

Sandbox

Slide

Small airplanes, automobiles, trucks, boats, trains

Small boards for building, hauling

Soap-bubble pipes

Solid child-size hammer, large nails, soft wood

Stove

Suitcases

Table and chair, child-size

Toy animals

Train, dump truck, steam shovel large enough for child to ride on

Tricycle

Wagon

Wheelbarrow

Wooden or rubber vehicles (auto, truck, ambulance, fire engine)

Wooden shoe for lacing

Books for
Three-Year-Olds

Adoff, Arnold. *Make a Circle. Keep Us In.* New York: Delacorte, 1975.

Brown, Margaret Wise. *The Indoor Noisy Book.* New York: Harper & Row, 1942.

———. *Shhh! Bang!* New York: Harper & Row, 1942.

———. *Goodnight Moon.* New York: Harper & Row, 1947.

———. *The Important Book.* New York: Harper & Row, 1949.

Buckley, Helen. *My Sister and I.* New York: Lothrop, Lee & Shepard, 1963.

———. *Grandmother and I.* New York: Lothrop, Lee & Shepard, 1965.

Cole, William. *What's Good for a Three Year Old?* New York: Holt, Rinehart, and Winston, 1971.

Duvoisin, Roger. *The Rain Puddle.* New York: Lothrop, Lee & Shepard, 1965.

———. *The Crocodile in the Tree.* New York: Knopf, 1973.

———. *Our Veronica Goes to Petunia Farm.* New York: Knopf/ Pantheon, 1973.

Emberly, Ed. *Klippity Klop.* Boston: Little, Brown, 1975.

Galdone, Paul (Illustrator). *Old Woman and Her Pig.* New York: McGraw-Hill, 1961.

———. *The Three Bears.* New York: Seabury, 1972.

Guilfoile, Elizabeth. *Nobody Listens to Andrew.* Chicago: Follett, 1962.

Hoban, Russell. *Bedtime for Frances.* New York: Harper & Row, 1960.

Keats, Ezra Jack. *Peter's Chair*. New York: Harper & Row, 1967.

Kessler, Ethel, and Kessler, Leonard. *The Big Red Bus*. Garden City, N.Y.: Doubleday, 1964.

Klein, Leonore. *Mud, Mud, Mud*. New York: Knopf, 1962.

Klein, Norma. *Girls Can Be Anything*. New York: Dutton, 1973.

Kraus, Ruth. *Happy Day*. New York: Harper & Row, 1949.

———. *The Backward Day*. New York: Harper & Row, 1950.

Kuskin, Karla. *All Sizes of Noises*. New York: Harper & Row, 1962.

Langstaff, Nancy. *A Tiny Baby For You*. New York: Harcourt Brace Jovanovich, 1955.

Levine, Joan Goldman. *A Bedtime Story*. New York: Dutton, 1975.

Lionni, Leo. *Little Blue and Little Yellow*. New York: Astor-Honor, 1959.

———. *Swimmy.* New York: Pantheon, 1963.

———. *The Biggest House in the World*. New York: Knopf/Pantheon, 1973.

Lobel, Arnold. *A Zoo for Mister Muster*. New York: Harper & Row, 1962.

McGovern, Ann. *Too Much Noise*. Boston: Houghton Mifflin, 1967.

Merriam, Eve. *Boys and Girls: Girls and Boys*. New York: Holt, Rinehart and Winston, 1972.

Moffett, Martha. *A Flower Pot Is Not a Hat*. New York: Dutton, 1972.

Nakano, Hirotaka. *Elephant Blue*. Indianapolis: Bobbs Merrill, 1970.

Nôdset, Joan L. *Who Took the Farmer's Hat?* New York: Harper & Row, 1963.

Parsons, Ellen. *Rainy Day Together*. New York: Harper & Row, 1971.

Paterson, Diane. *Eat*. New York: Dial, 1975.

Petie, Harriet. *Billions of Bugs*. Englewood Cliffs, N.J.: Prentice-Hall, 1975.

Ray, Wade. *A Train to Spain*. New York: Knopf, 1963.

Ringi, Kjell. *The Sun and the Cloud*. New York: Harper & Row, 1971.

Schick, Eleanor. *A Surprise in the Forest*. New York: Harper & Row, 1964.

Seuss, Dr. *The Cat in the Hat*. New York: Random House, 1957.

———. *The Foot Book*. New York: Random House, 1968.

Simon, Norma. *The Baby House*. Philadelphia: Lippincott, 1955.

Skaar, Grace. *What Do Animals Say?* New York: Young Scott, 1968.

Skorpen, Liesel Moak. *Outside My Window*. New York: Harper & Row, 1968.

Stein, Sara Bonnett. *Making Babies*. New York: Walker, 1975.

Tudor, Tasha. *Pumpkin Moonshine*. New York: Walck, 1962.

Udry, Janice. *A Tree Is Nice*. New York: Harper & Row, 1956.

Williams, Margery. *The Velveteen Rabbit*. Garden City, N.Y.: Doubleday, 1958.

Zion, Gene. *Really Spring*. New York: Harper & Row, 1956.

Zolotow, Charlotte. *Do You Know What I'll Do?* New York: Harper & Row, 1958.

———. *The Three Funny Friends*. New York: Harper & Row, 1961.

———. *William's Doll*. New York: Harper & Row, 1972.

———. *Hold My Hand*. New York: Harper & Row, 1973.

Books for the Parents
of Three-Year-Olds

Ames, Louise Bates. *Parents Ask.* A syndicated daily newspaper column. New Haven, Conn.: Gesell Institute, 1952–.
———. *Child Care and Development.* Philadelphia: Lippincott, 1970.
Ames, Louise Bates, and Chase, Joan Ames. *Don't Push Your Preschooler.* New York: Harper & Row, 1974.
Braga, Laurie, and Braga, Joseph. *Learning and Growing: A Guide to Child Development.* New York: Prentice-Hall, 1975.
Brazelton, T. Berry. *Infants and Mothers.* New York: Delacorte, 1969.
———. *Toddlers and Their Parents.* New York: Delacorte, 1974.
Caplan, Frank, and Caplan, Theresa. *The Power of Play.* New York: Doubleday, 1973.
Cleveland, Anne. *Parent from Zero to Ten.* New York: Simon & Schuster, 1958.
Coffin, Patricia. *1, 2, 3, 4, 5, 6. How to Understand and Enjoy the Years That Count.* New York: Macmillan, 1972.
Comer, James P., and Poussaint, Alvin F. *Black Child Care.* New York: Simon & Schuster, 1975.
Crook, William G. *Can Your Child Read? Is He Hyperactive?* Jackson, Tenn.: Pedicenter Press, 1975.
Dodson, Fitzhugh. *How to Parent.* Los Angeles: Nash, 1970.
———. *How to Father.* Los Angeles: Nash, 1974.
Feingold, Ben J. *Why Your Child Is Hyperactive.* New York: Random House, 1975.

158

Forer, Lucille K. *Birth Order and Life Roles.* Springfield, Ill.: C. C. Thomas, 1969.

Gardner, Richard A. *Understanding Children.* New York: Aronson, 1973.

Gersh, Marvin J. *How to Raise Children at Home in Your Spare Time.* New York: Stein & Day, 1966.

Gesell, Arnold; Ilg, Frances L.; and Ames, Louise B. *Infant and Child in the Culture of Today.* New York: Harper & Row, rev. ed., 1974.

Grollman, Earl A. (Ed.) *Explaining Divorce to Children.* Boston: Beacon Press, 1969.

———. *Explaining Death to Children.* Boston: Beacon Press, 1967.

Hartley, Ruth E., and Goldensen, Robert M. *The Complete Book of Children's Play.* New York: Crowell, 1970.

Holt, L. Emmett, Jr. *Good Housekeeping Book of Baby and Child Care.* New York: Appleton-Century-Crofts, 1957.

Ilg, Frances L.; Ames, Louise B.; Goodenough, Evelyn; and Andresen, Irene. *The Gesell Institute Party Book.* New York: Harper & Row, 1959.

———. *Child Behavior.* New York: Harper & Row, 1957.

Johnson, June. *Home Play for the Preschool Child.* New York: Harper & Row, 1957.

LeShan, Eda. *How to Survive Parenthood.* New York: Random House, 1965.

Liepmann, Lise. *Your Child's Sensory World.* New York: Dial, 1973.

McIntire, Roger W. *For Love of Children.* Del Mar, Calif.: CRM Books, 1970.

Maynard, Fredelle. *Guiding Your Child to a More Creative Life.* New York: Doubleday, 1973. (Contains excellent lists of books for parents on arts and crafts: drawing, painting, crayoning, clay modeling, ceramics, fabrics and yarns, puppets, also children's records.)

Pitcher, Evelyn G., and Ames, Louise B. *The Guidance Nursery School.* New York: Harper & Row, rev. ed., 1975.

Smith, Lendon H. *The Children's Doctor.* Englewood Cliffs, N.J.: Prentice-Hall, 1969.

———. *Improving Your Child's Behavior Chemistry.* New York: Prentice-Hall, 1976.

Toman, Walter. *Family Constellation: Its Effect on Personality and Social Behavior.* New York: Springer, 1969.

Weisberger, Eleanor. *Your Young Child and You.* New York: E. P. Dutton, 1975.

Wender, Paul H. *The Hyperactive Child: A Guide for Parents.* New York: Crown, 1973.

Wunderlich, Ray. *Allergy, Brains and Children Coping.* St. Petersburg, Fla.: Johnny Reads Press, 1973.

Young, Milton A. *Buttons Are to Push.* New York: Pitman, 1970.

NOTES

1. This information was provided by Richard J. Apell, O.D., director of the Visual Department of the Gesell Institute of Child Development.
2. The Incomplete Man Test was introduced as a preschool test by Dr. Arnold Gesell in the 1920s. It consists of the printed figure of a man with one arm and hand, one leg and foot, head, one side of the neck and half a tie, one ear, hair on one side of the head, nose, and mouth. The only part for which a model is not provided is the eye. The child is asked to complete this figure. As children grow older, they add more and more parts to the man, and the parts are increasingly accurate. This has proved to be one of the most effective of our developmental tests for determining the *behavior age* of the child.
3. Here we emphasize the kinds of things children play with, rather than child-child interaction in play as earlier, on pages 13 to 25.
4. In order to make use of a controlled situation, our observations were made during the course of the Gesell Preschool Examination, as described in *The First Five Years of Life*, by Arnold Gesell et al. (New York: Harper & Row, 1940). This examination was given individually to boys and girls of each of the preschool ages.
5. Laurie Braga and Joseph Braga, *Learning and Growing: A Guide to Child Development* (Englewood Cliffs, N.J.: Prentice-Hall, 1975).
6. Among the physicians who have written helpful and informative books on the damaging effects that can come from a harmful diet are Drs. William Crook, Ben J. Feingold, Lendon H. Smith, and Ray Wunderlich, whose books are listed on pages 158 and 159.

• *Notes* •

7. For a specific discussion of visual behavior at Three, see pages 45 to 46.
8. Louise B. Ames, *Children's Stories*, Genetic Psychology Monographs 73 (1966): 337–396.
9. Dr. Sheldon's systematic treatment of the various personality characteristics that have been found to accompany different kinds of physical structure is discussed in brief in a companion volume, *Your Four-Year-Old*, by Louise B. Ames and Frances L. Ilg (New York: Delacorte, 1976).
10. Stella Chess et al., *Your Child Is a Person* (New York: Viking, 1965).
11. Arnold Gesell, "The Stability of Mental-Growth Careers," *Thirty-ninth Yearbook of the National Society for the Study of Education*, part 2 (Bloomington, Ill.: Public School Publishing Co., 1940).

INDEX

Photo Credits